REVIEWS FOR

CW00701840

HALF-FORGOTTEN THINGS

Just finished reading memories of this Aberásturi house in the book Half-Forgotten Things by Txomin and Nilda Aberásturi. I couldn't sleep, I laughed and cried. Thanks to them for this treasure.
Leo Escaño

Same here. I laughed and cried. I was telling my daughter over the phone about the Coromina brothers, about Tito Ed and Tito Lito, how they were willing to die as long as their loved ones would be spared. I told her that's true love. I learned so many lessons from the book, too, from Lolo Dioni:"You could not be perfect, nobody is; all you could do is try. Do not put too much value on financial success, but rather strive to be a decent human being, caring and kind and honest, a person with integrity." Also that in case there are misunderstandings, the parties concerned should do everything, talk things out, communicate as soon as possible, before it's too late. One of the lines I will never forget was Lolo Onsoy's words:"I lost my right hand, my loyal companion, my best friend."
Mercedes Veloso Rafanan

A sensitive and loving portrayal of a close-knit family. A fascinating memoir about ordinary people and their extraordinary life story set against the backdrop of an idyllic milieu, soon shattered by that most tragic event of modern times, the WWII. Reminds one of Russell Baker's book "Growing Up" – filled with comedic scenes and interspersed with pathos - all collected in a single strand of a story written with a loving hand. Leaves the reader more appreciative of life, love and family. Could hardly put down the book.
Leopoldo Gonzaga Anoche
Department Chair
Southville Foreign University

I truly enjoyed reading this book. I learnt a lot about family that I never heard before. The adventures of Tito Titing and Tito Otic were so hilarious, but the story about Tito Ed, his brother Tito Lito, and Tita Lolita were so heartbreaking. I can only imagine the dinner parties at the Villa hosted by Lolo Onsoy and Lola Peling that Tito Txomin looked forward to. The good old days. Lolo Dioni was truly a man of great qualities. He was an inspiration. Congratulations to Tita Nilda and Tito Txomin for this wonderful work!
Ramon Escaño Aberásturi

A very well-written book.
Alfredo Asuncion

The Aberásturis and Malitbog were unknown entities until Txomin and Nilda Aberásturi gave them life in an engaging and well-written distillation of the travails and triumphs of an astonishing family. The memoir takes us to a distant time and place but could be today's story because human emotions transcend time and the Aberásturis had no shortage of the foibles and their gifts, the joys and their pathos shared among the wide array of characters depicted in the narrative. The anecdotes of family gatherings and inevitable strife and scandals resonate so well I feel the Aberásturis were my family, too.
Jess N. San Agustin

I heard stories from my father (Ramon Aberásturi) but there are still so many stories here that I have the privilege of knowing and understanding now. I believe history is very important for us to know our families better and to know who we really are.
The book is written in such a manner that it is so vivid, you can really picture yourself in some situations. Overall, it captures a lot of emotions, happiness, sadness and it is definitely heartwarming
Cristina Aberásturi Ducloux

The best thing about this book is that the heroes and the good guys are your own family. I haven't met most of these people in the book, but to know their bravery, honour and inspiring virtue still makes me proud to have come from such a family. Thank you Lolo Txomin and Lola Nilda for creating this memoir.

Cristina Lopez Gaston

I'm the grandson of Cristina and the son of Dioni. This is an excellent book. I wish I could meet more of our family.

Tonito Lopez

The authors Nilda and Txomin Aberásturi bring to life not only memories of an extraordinary chapter in the life of Txomin, a member of a prominent Spanish Basque family in Southern Leyte, but also vividly depict the color, smell and sound of Malitbog.

The book has certainly provided the reader a window into an age "Almost Forgotten" and yet will instead be long remembered.

It is particularly fascinating to read excerpts of real life events that are both personal and familiar to me. Otik Escaño, Juaning Escaño and Tintoy Aberásturi were my "barkada" too, and this book instilled a deep sense of loss and nostalgia for an era gone by.

For all of this, I thank you.

Dr. Raul "Dodong" Sala
Clinical Professor, Albert Einstein College of Medicine, New York.
Diplomate, America Board of PMR
"Son" of Malitbog

Review of Half-Forgotten Things
Nostalgic, witty, funny
By *Verified* Amazon Customer   on August 29, 2016

Nostalgic, witty and funny. What a remarkable love letter to a small town in southern Philippines. Written with affection, it got those who know the place longing to go back to it. This true story is like a charming tale of the verdant countryside and white beaches, the lusty neighborhoods and the sweet secrets of its townspeople, all intermingled with the gentleness and foibles of its families. A good read indeed. It also helps that the writing is crisp and lush, like the time that it was before the Great War. There are lots of things in this small book: pathos, scandals, hilarity, passion, and of course, love; but the book is also an evocative reflection on a place of one's youth that is long gone but whose bittersweet memories still linger on, like a feeling of great forlornness. I just love this book.

HALF-FORGOTTEN THINGS
Vignettes From A Life

A Memoir By

TXOMIN ABERÁSTURI

AND

NILDA ABERÁSTURI

New York
August 2010

Cover photo by Ton Darlucio

Back cover text by Susan Astor

Available from Amazon.com and other retail outlets
Available on Kindle and online stores

This book is a tribute to my father,

Dionisio Aberásturi,

as upright a human being as
I could ever hope to find,
whose footprints he left in my life
I never filled,
but I became a better man,
a more decent man,
because of them.

Txomin Aberásturi
New York, 2006

To Txomin
best friend
who was always so sure I could
when I was sure I couldn't
and without whom.............

I gratefully acknowledge the following:

The Edna St. Vincent Millay Society
Through Elizabeth Barnett
for permission to reprint lines from *Sonnet III* - *Renascence*
by Edna St. Vincent Millay

Lines from **All The Things You Are**
From Very Warm For May
Lyrics by Oscar Hammerstein II
Music by Jerome Kern
Copyright © 1939 UNIVERSAL-POLYGRAM INTERNATIONAL
  PUBLISHING, INC.
Copyright Renewed
All Rights Reserved
Reprinted by Permission of Hal Leonard Corporation

The US Naval Institute Press
for permission to excerpt pages from
Battle of Leyte Gulf
23-26 October 1944
By Thomas J. Cutler

Tim Lanzendörfer
for allowing me to "use any way you want"
pages from his article
Glorious Death: The Battle of Leyte Gulf
October 23-25, 1944

You go no more on your exultant feet
Up paths that only mist and morning knew,
Or watch the wind, or listen to the beat
Of a bird's wings too high in air to view,--
But you were something more than young and sweet
And fair,--and the long year remembers you.

III - Renascence

Edna St. Vincent Millay

Also by Nilda Aberásturi

When Shadows Fall
A Novel

The Constant Heart
Book-in-Progress

memory is fleeting
catch it before it flies irretrievably away

I have taken certain liberties with names and dates
in respect to family members I care about deeply,
but the story remains true
to my remembrance of this time in my past.

Txomin Aberásturi
New York

Map of Malitbog, Southern Leyte
Philippines

Map of Forua
Spain

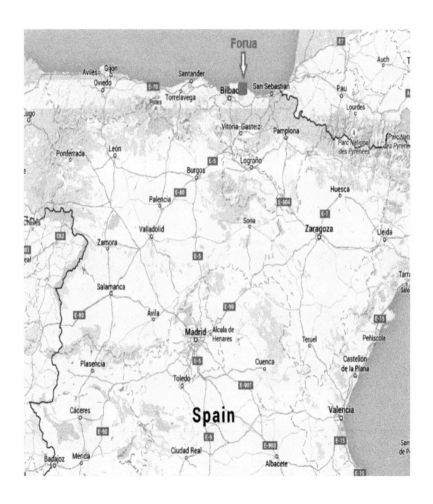

1

The jeep wound down the mountain road and the sea loomed before us, shining bright against the sun, the movements on its surface glinting points of dazzling light, white stars bouncing off the water as they caught the morning sun. This was the route I liked to take coming home after a long absence, through the raw roads that cut through the craggy mountain, past groves of bamboo standing forlorn in open fields, their reedy stems swaying to whichever way the winds chose to whip them; the diplomat of plants, still rooted to the spot where they had stood for decades, while other neighbors, with trunks more sturdy but unyielding, had long been uprooted by sweeping winds of typhoons that frequent these parts. We passed scattered communities of bamboo houses with thatched roofs of *nipa* palm, their front yards swept neat by coconut-midrib brooms, flowers leaning against bamboo fences, women sitting on bamboo stairs braiding their daughters' hair, men squatting by the roadside, stroking the feathers of fighting cocks, unmindful of time, in no hurry to go anywhere, do anything, patterns of life familiar in settlements in these rural towns.

The rain the night before had washed the morning white. After the rains, the rice fields flourished full and green and lush, and the earth awakened to the cacophony of frogs' greetings and small birds fluttering their small-bird wings as they piped their songs. Sunlight speared through rice stalks standing knee-deep in water, while the scent of rice ripening in long stretches still stormed the senses, as it always did here. With the rains came the down-to-earth politics of bumps from rain-puddled, potholed roads, asphalted only on elections years, abusing our behinds in the family jeep, which I called 'the little green jeep that can' because even with its top overflowing with luggage, and its inside crammed with seven people, it nevertheless swallowed up the kilometers with ease, bumping and swaying to noisy talk and laughter.

But I was alone today, and the non-stop chatter of the garrulous driver could not intrude into my thoughts, full of memories as they were, after being away for a long time. After a while, we left the mountain road and took the highway. The road was not as bad here, was better maintained, and travel did not take as long. In a few minutes we entered the town, this place where I was born and grew up, this town that held captive the hearts of everyone who came here, even though, like me, they had left it behind a long while back.

Malitbog. It had always eluded time, held back the years, waking from sleep briefly when jolted by an occasional upheaval-- a scandal here, a war there, the periodic typhoons that left havoc in their wake: uprooting trees, ripping off roofs, changing the course of rivers, even of lives--and always contrived to rise from the ruins, back on its feet, somehow managing to look exactly the same.

Malitbog. A singular, private little town on the southern end of the island of Leyte, its one reluctant claim to fame the fictional book *An American Guerilla in the Philippines*, which was set here, the heroine of the book modeled after one of my cousins. The province, too, lays claim to a piece of history: the first Mass ever held on Philippine soil by the Spaniard Ferdinand Magellan when he discovered the country some five hundred years before. Then there's the greatest naval battle ever fought in history, the Battle of Leyte Gulf during the Second World War, which took place off these shores.

Time stood still here; no matter how long or far away I strayed, it always looked the same when I returned. The houses along the roads were still there, their yards neatly tended, the white, yellow and lavender blossoms of the frangipani and oleander trees a riot of colors crowning the leaves, droplets of last night's rain still shivering on their edges, waiting for a breeze to breathe them down into a soft shower. The wooden bridges still stood, the waters meandering or rushing under them as clear and as cold as when I, a small boy barefoot and in short pants, waded through them, pocketing stones and rocks and varied twigs and such.

Like me, most young members of my family, and indeed of the town, had moved on to other places, other countries and endeavors. Only the older folks stayed, and those too steeped in their ways, too content or too complacent to change habits, shift places or breach traditions. I lived and worked in the city now, but somehow I had not absorbed the sophistication that a cosmopolitan city offered; it seemed I never left this place and it never left me.

The cemetery appeared before us, white and desolate but strangely comforting, welcoming me as it always did when I roamed far.

"Would you like to visit your father first?" the driver asked, waking me from my reverie. Like the other drivers, and indeed the others the family employed, he had worked with us for as long as I could remember, driving one or another of the many trucks that serviced the family business, or the jeeps that catered to the various needs of family members. He came to us before my father first bought a jeep, and stayed even after that jeep became old and dilapidated and was retired to the back of the house, picked bare of its remaining useful parts, and its skeleton hauled away and other jeeps took its place.

The driver did not wait for my answer. He swerved the jeep into the cemetery and parked at the mouth of the entrance, the wheels crunching the stones beneath. It was a cemetery like many others in small towns in the land: overcrowded, weed-grown, taken care of once a year on All Souls' Day. Most of the graves had headstones of cement. A few, tucked away on the edges, were marked with wooden crosses; the names painted on them had seeped away with weather and time. Now they looked sadly makeshift, as though they did not intend to stay long, as though they knew that if nobody came to re-stake their claims and paint the names back on again, the present tenants would have to gather themselves up and seek other beds, and new owners would take their places, and fresher crosses would mark them.

It was a cemetery like other cemeteries in small towns in the land, but for the imposing mausoleum that rose at the end of the cement pathway. The Escaño mausoleum, a marble rotunda rising some dozen steps from the ground, with an imposing relief of the Last Supper and a life-sized, life-like, white marble *Pieta* imported from Rome guarding its entrance. Niches with marble tablets were neatly arranged in the lower portion that now housed departed Escaño family members, a proud monument now become a tourist attraction.

It had its ghosts, this mausoleum, ghosts so accustomed to the living that they roamed around even in broad daylight. Once, when we had our pictures taken on the steps and the pictures were developed, one showed a shadow, an unmistakable silhouette against the sky, of *somebody* standing behind us.

The driver and I walked to the end of the path, past the mausoleum. We rounded the corner and there at the back was my father's burial ground, the cement top of his grave jutting a foot above the grass. The iron link that laced around the tomb was still shiny new, the ground well cared for. Save for a couple of other graves set way out, my father was sole occupant of this lonely sweep of land, wide as the eyes could see, whipped desolate by frequent roving winds, with the frangipani trees at his feet and sundry flowers at his head for company.

The frangipani blossoms the winds had lashed loose lay like fragrant offerings strewn on top of the grave. I swept them away with my hand, and read my father's name and the dates of his birth and death: Dionisio Aberásturi Endieza, October 9, 1885 - July 23, 1955. My family had planned a big celebration for his seventieth birthday, with my sisters and their families coming home for the event. But two months shy, the life he chose to live uneventfully was cut short by a death more bizarre than what he would have preferred had he a say in these matters.

A June gust warmed my face as I said a little prayer for him, dragging at first, but once begun, the words came tumbling out of the depths of my memory.

We passed the church and the convent on the way home, past the street lined with ancient acacia trees. When my sisters Cristina and Juanita were little, they used to swing from the sweeping branches that now stretched to the sky, their dark leaves a canopy shading the square and the street.

From the gate I could see our house, looming large at the end of the long driveway. My father had this house built when I was three years old. It had stood defiant for more than a quarter of a century, withstanding the years, weathering the typhoons that battered it, resisting even the termites that must have gotten their teeth yanked out from gnawing on the hardwood that Father used to build this house. I jumped out of the jeep, opened the gate and walked the length of the driveway, the driver and the jeep trailing behind me.

I had put in the stone walk on the driveway myself, after I graduated from college, while waiting for the results of the mechanical engineering board examinations. I was drunk the night before the exams, and took the board in a groggy fog. I celebrated constantly after graduation---carried a load of engineering review books all the weeks before the exams, intending, but never getting, to read them---and did not take the board review. My sister Juanita, still awake reading when I came home in the wee hours after long nights out, looked up from her book one night. "You know what," she said, "I shall have your statue erected on the front lawn should you pass that engineering board." Well, I did pass. Maybe one day that statue will rise from amongst the flowers and the stones!

A veritable woodland, green and lush, surrounded the house and grounds. Fruits hung heavy on various fruit trees; avocados dangled from branches, waiting to be plucked. Some, impatient, dropped to the ground where we would find them, camouflaged like chameleons, nestled green on the green grass. The guavas had always been as prolific as various family members, assuaging cravings for fruit through various pregnancies. A couple of *rambutan* trees and the mango tree and its mate stood barren still. Too occupied with bearing children, the family had never been able to coax fruits from them.

Clusters of orchids clung wild to trunks of tamarind trees, and filled the church with white when my sister Clotilde got married. Oleanders, crepe myrtle, and gardenias crowded both sides of the driveway.

Fat leaves and brilliant flowers of various classes of begonias spilled out of their boxes on the porch. We used to congregate here in the early afternoons and tell stories until the sun went down and mosquitoes came out of their sleeping places driving us into the house.

The door was unlocked, as though waiting for me. I stepped inside and was engulfed by the coolness of the large living room and its memories. The piano stood against one wall. I could still hear my sisters Juanita playing a favorite Chopin waltz, the *Number Nine,* and Emiliana singing *El Reloj.* The bust of the Sacred Heart of Jesus, screwed on the wall, looked down from above the piano, reigning over the statues of lesser saints on the piano top. I saw a reedy imp of a boy that was me, bare feet and yellow hair, hair dyed gold by countless suns, and my brother Ramon, three years older but much bigger, kneeling in front of that piano. When he and I fought---fights that were always instigated by me---my mother made us go down on our knees in front of these saints to ask for forgiveness. Depending on the gravity of our sins, she would make us kneel with both arms outstretched, a book on each open palm, or kneel on *mongo* beans scattered on the wooden floor. The moment she turned her back, we would slowly put the books down, or wipe off the beans that clung obstinately to our knees. After a minute of pondering our transgressions, I would inch nearer my brother and poke him in the ribs with my elbow. Not to be outdone, he would poke me with his. This would go on until we erupted in laughter and Mother invented more drastic punishments or, ragged from the antics of an irrepressible instigator and his brother who did not need much instigating, she drove us outside to play. "And don't come up unless you're bleeding," she would say, years before I read this line in the *Reader's Digest.*

The hardwood floors gleamed, kept that way by two housemaids whose sole responsibility was to keep the living room and the bedrooms in perfect order. They wore old socks over their hands like gloves so as not to leave prints on the surfaces while they dusted and waxed and mopped until every inch glowed. Sometimes, when the morning sun flooded the rooms, I could catch my reflection on the floors, a vague me, pulled tall and long

7   Half-Forgotten Things
         Vignettes From A Life

or pressed fat and short, sometimes leaf-dappled across, most times distorted and misshapen, depending on which way the light played on the wood. As children, we were not allowed to stay in the living room during the day, unless we were on our knees, contemplating our sins in front of those saints.

The bookshelves dominated one far side of the room, going up from floor to ceiling, still crammed with books. Reading is a passion in this family. Sometimes, far unto the night, I would hear one sister or another laughing out loud, deriving more enjoyment from books than from sleep. We had more books than the local library, spilling from shelves to floors, volumes upon volumes, well-handled, fully savored, most read many times. Cousins and friends would drop by to pick up one or two, and leave behind scraps of current events, the local news, and inevitably, the latest gossip.

2

Mother came out from her bedroom to greet me. Tall and slim, she always held her head high, and with her hair in a chic chignon, always looked quite regal. This is how I always remember her, elegantly turned out, smelling of one of the French perfumes that my sisters supplied her, wearing some pieces of jewelry that she owned for as long as I could remember. Today, she was wearing one of the silk dresses and a Chanel perfume my sister Cristina sent her. Cristina sent whatever she thought my parents needed, more than just silks and perfumes--once a refrigerator, another time a car, a green Austin sedan, which matched the color of the house, the refrigerator, the jeep, all in various shades of green, Mother's favorite color.

Mother was always up and about by dawn. By the time the house had wakened, she was already seated at the round table in the small dining room, waiting breakfast for us, already dressed up for the day, her hair brushed back from her face, her jewelry in place, smoking one of the *cigarillos* she herself rolled.

She never took naps after lunch as we did, and on afternoons when the house slept, she listened to her radio while she fashioned her own cigarettes from a strip of tobacco rolled in a square of *buri* leaf. When little, I would wake up before the others did and find her where she always was at this time of day, rolling her cigarettes, putting her handiwork neatly in a box. This was also story-telling time, hours I loved, when she told me stories about her youth, about the family. She would light a cigarette, stick it in my mouth, light another one for herself and we would share quiet moments, telling stories or just puffing away.

- - - -

"Church?" I asked as I kissed her, noting the printed silk dress, one of the many that she wore only when she went out. Mother liked to arrange things neatly in compartments---silk dresses for going out, cotton dresses for the house; up by 6, quiet moments to herself after lunch, dinner at 8.

"Yes," she answered. "Come with me?" She never wanted to take the jeep when she went to church, preferring to walk instead. I dismissed the driver and she took my arm as we walked to church together. I had been away a long time and she had sent me the money for the fare so I would be sure to spend this week at home.

Shafts of morning sunlight filtered like crystal shards through the leaves of the giant acacia trees lining the street, casting lights and shadows that trembled on the asphalt. I took deep breaths of the air that somehow smelled different here, smells of morning and grass and the sea a few feet away.

On the other side of the road, from across the town plaza, I could see the sea, dazzling in the morning sun, waves frothing and foaming as they hit the shore, the sound as they slapped the sand the somnolent rhythm that swayed me to sleep on countless sick-child nights. Father taught us to swim when we were still very young. He would take us to the pier and would urge us to jump while he waited for us in the water. At first he would catch us right away, then make us swim on our own while he stayed right beside us. Later, when we became less hesitant and more confident, he would watch as we jumped from the pier, watch us sink into the water, then break out of the surface, padding the swells like puppies, coughing out water, laughing, triumphant, as he knew we would.

I started a love affair with this stretch of water at an early age; this temptation in my young life that was hardest to resist, a siren song calling to me inside the schoolhouse, drowning my teacher's voice, refusing to let go until heeded. I would gaze longingly at the direction of the sea; think of the tide I knew would be high. Oh, well, I would tell myself, teacher had already lost me, I might as well go. I would raise one hand as if asking permission to go to the bathroom, but instead would sprint the hundred or so acacia-tree-shaded yards to the wharf, and jump into the salty coolness. I would go under with my eyes wide open, check seaweeds floating in front of my face, stare down a fish staring at me, extend my hand swiftly to grasp it, watch as it would wiggle away. I would burst out of the water to catch my breath, feeling free, exhilarated, then plunge back down again, do underwater cartwheels, and just forget the time, until a servant sent out by my mother would call me from my watery bliss.

"Txomin, Txomin." I was six years old, the sun shone bright in the sky; the saltwater felt good on my body, nothing else mattered.

But the servant was persistent. "Txomin, Txomin, if you don't come home now, your Mama will come and get you herself." What a blatant lie. Mother would never get out of the house just to get me. I could hide underwater and ignore that strident voice, but the servant would not leave until she heard from me and I could not stay submerged for long. I had to come up for air and she knew it.

Mother would fuss, shoo me to the bathroom where my sister Clotilde waited. She would scour the salt off my body with the hated washcloth, stick it deep into my ears, soap my hair, and with long arms, wash me down until I was free of soap and blue in the face. I would squirm and writhe and struggle to be free from those long arms, flail my shorter ones, and shake water all over the bathroom like a protesting dog. To no avail.

The next day, my teacher would tell on me, and for cutting classes, Mother would beat my legs with a midrib of a coconut palm that she kept away for leg-beating time, her punishment of choice for our misbehavior, mostly mine. "Mama," I would plead, "just use your slippers, please, please." Her slippers that were made of soft abaca. "Slippers don't hurt and won't teach you a lesson," she would say.

This was the kind of discipline she imposed in our house. When I, or my brother Ramon, came home from school and complained that our teacher made us do a lot of work, or took any such measures teachers called discipline, or sometimes even rapping our wrists when we misbehaved, my mother never took our side. "Hey, you are even too much for me, and there are only two of you. Think how hard it is for that poor teacher, with so many children she has to deal with." Or, dismissingly, "*Merece*. I'm sure you deserved it." I was sure I did, too, so there the matter always rested.

-    -   -   -

I am the youngest of four sisters and a brother, and was sickly. Father had an edict in our house: I was not to be touched. When I needed discipline, he said, he would do it himself, which he, a large man stern and strong, with principles that were never negotiable except where my punishment was concerned, very seldom did. This decree went over Mother's head, however, and she never spared the coconut-midrib rod. Today, this might be called child abuse. When and where I grew up, the rod, no matter the make, was the bedrock of discipline that, if spared, spoiled the child. But the sting of Mother's flimsy switch, though it sent me jumping up and down when it hit my legs, was fleeting and forgettable, trying my dignity more than my legs. So many years and so many coconut midribs later, and here I was, still uncured of my love affair with this stretch of water.

We passed the schoolhouse where I spent the first years of my school life. I learned my letters here, not as swiftly as I learned my numbers, taught me by my teacher Ma'am Sanches. Even though she always told Mother of my sins in the classroom, Ma'am Sanches was still my favorite teacher. Any grown woman who had more energy than I had in those days always inspired awe in me.

Friday afternoons after class, she went straight from school to the house of Na Juling. There she played *mahjong* from Friday night to Monday morning, three nights and two days, straight. Monday morning, we came to class and joy of joys! no teacher. We would take our time in boisterous relief before going out to search for her, marching happily over to Na Juling's house where we knew she would be. "Ma'am Sanches," we would ask hopefully, "we are not going to have classes this morning, are we?"

But she always dashed our hopes. "You go right ahead," she would say, "I'll be there in a little while." She would be late---a bit sleepy, very cranky---but that was all right with us. A few minutes of reprieve from the humdrum of classes were always welcome.

The schoolhouse, abandoned now, looked old and decrepit. Rain, weather and time had leached into the grain of the wood. Windowpanes, once firm and solid enough to hold inside children wanting to burst free, now drooped in silence. Slats of lumber boarded up the windows. Were they ever painted? I could not now recall. The iron rails that used to keep the outside world firmly out were long gone. So were the ravaged faces that looked out those windows, faces of the men held prisoners there during the war, faces that looked out hopefully for bits and pieces of news of the world they had left behind, a world that seemed to recede farther away from their grasp, listening for voices that held shades of laughter, glimmer of hope, laughter that for a long time had not been their luxury to hear, holding to hope that, little by little, they were running short of, enduring in those dark, dank rooms that were the last spaces they would occupy in this lifetime, in that time that we called The War Time.

Straight ahead, at the end of the road, the church shone, a new coat of white on her cement walls. Like those acacia trees that lined the street, that church had always been there, ever since I could remember, had seen baptisms and weddings and had bidden many a dead goodbye.

The convent stood near the church, dapper, too, with its own new coat of white. We had a new assistant parish priest, fresh out of the seminary, a young, enthusiastic whirlwind who repaired, repainted and raised funds for new additions. "New broom, you know," confided my sisters. Sweeps cleaner.

We had an old broom of a priest here. Father Isong was not too old, really, just too weary, too preoccupied, his concerns not with matters too spiritual. His mother went with him to every parish he was assigned to, keeping house for him, managing his convent, managing him. At that age he was still trying to break loose from her maternal skirt, and, sadly, not succeeding.

All he wanted was to get away. As soon as he finished saying his last Mass of the morning, he waited outside the church and boarded the first passenger bus that passed by. Whether it went north or south did not matter much to Father Isong. The thing was to get on the bus and go. What thoughts he had while inside the bus nobody knew. He just sat there until the last point of the bus' destination, and then he boarded the last bus back to our town. Once, when he did not appear at the convent after Mass and left his mother stewing, waiting breakfast, and then lunch, for him, his mother swore she had enough. When he walked up the convent steps in time for supper, she whacked him with a broom.

He did not stay long in our parish, but he left such a mark in our town that children who tended to roam were likened to him. "Another Father Isong in the making," people would say.

- - - -

We were early and the church was still dimly lit. The assistant parish priest came out from the recesses of the building to greet us. He regaled us with small talk, until the bells proclaimed the start of Mass.

The church smelled of candles when we came in, candles and incense and whatever else gave churches their own peculiar sacred smells. This had always been a sanctuary for me, this old church. Troubled, I would sit in the anonymity of the last pew, empty my thoughts, let the stillness wash over me, and leave the church somehow at peace. Today, the priest was young and impatient, the sermon was short, and Mass lasted a scant thirty minutes.

On Sundays and holy days, however, when Masses were celebrated by Father Quimbo, the parish priest, Masses could run on well over an hour, with the sermon taking up the bulk of the minutes. These were the parish priest's days---Sundays and holy days, with two Masses in the morning and one in the afternoon, when the church was filled with captive parishioners. Whether they listened or they entertained themselves with their own flights of daydreams did not matter; they were rooted to their seats, nothing could budge them, nothing they could do but stay. Once in a while, Father Quimbo would stress a point with a booming voice, and a soft rustle would ensue, as they were jolted back to the tiresome present. In those days, priests said Mass facing the altar, their backs to the congregation. When Father Quimbo turned around to give a blessing, he would crane his neck and scan the length and breadth of the church. My cousin Otic Escaño swore that with that one long look, he knew who was absent from Mass. "*Honest to God, true story*," Otic would answer our skeptical looks. Before next Sunday rolled around, those slothful souls avoided passing by the church lest Father Quimbo would espy them and they would get a heavy dose of his sarcasm.

Father Quimbo was in his element when he had issues with Sunday collections. He had a big voice and shamed his parishioners from his pulpit. "I found coins in the collection last Sunday. Coins! Next time," here he would lower his voice to achieve a theatrical note, "please just keep your coins to yourselves. I am sure you need them more than your Church does."

His voice was just as loud in his confessional as it was from his pulpit, meting out advice and penance to penitents that carried way outside his confessional box, that his flock would rather *not sin* than endure a verbal, public lashing. Women, it seemed, bore the brunt of his ire more than did men, maybe because his women parishioners were more scrupulous in their confessions, readily accepting culpability in pleasures ("If it feels good it's a sin, if it feels very good, it's a mortal sin.") that men savor with little pangs of guilt that did not have to be brought to a confessor's attention ("What does your conscience say?").

"Don't you have anything better to do than read those bad books?" Father Quimbo would scold the women loudly. "Books with all those sex in them will lead you to sin. Read the Bible instead, read your prayer book." Or, "Birth control thwarts God's will and is a big sin. A *biiiig* sin. Abstain if you must, but remember, it is a sin, too, to deny your husband his conjugal rights." The confused sinner would slink out of the curtains of his confessional, conscious of eyes boring on her, more ashamed than repentant. And so others squeezed as much from the wide range that *conscience* allowed them. "I don't confess every single sin I have," declared Floro, our neighbor, in his feminine voice, "I just confess the beautiful ones," with a feathery flourish of his hand, dramatically tossing back his hair, and did not leave much to the imagination as to what the unbeautiful sins were.

Anyway, we were a God-fearing tribe. A potent tribe, too, that no method of birth control could restrain, producing children by the dozens. The only birth control sanctioned by the church, according to Father Quimbo, who ruled our souls with an iron hand, was the rhythm method--abstinence from sex when the wife was fertile. This never worked for us. The Aberásturi sperm was potent and relentless, ferreting out the egg hiding there somewhere. Sometimes, though, the men strayed from the straight and narrow paths hammered out by Father Quimbo, stepped out of bounds and went the unsanctioned ways of the artificial birth control, which were a laugh. Take my cousin Kits, for instance, who must have tried all birth control methods available to man, but already had one shy of a dozen children, trying the spermicidal jelly, which was a hoot, really, needing at least fifteen minutes to work. "Is it time already?" he asked his wife. "Not yet," she said. After a couple of minutes: "Is it time already?" "Not yet," from his wife. After another couple of minutes, very annoyed now: "Isn't it time yet?" But a watched kettle never boils, as the old cliché would tell you. "Just keep still there," replied the equally annoyed wife, "I'll tell you when it is." Then when it was time: "It's time, Kits." "Forget it," would come the exasperated reply from under the pillows, "I don't want to anymore."

And condoms, well, forget condoms. "Oy, what the hell is this?" trying it on this way, then trying it on that way, grumbling all the while, spontaneous desire fading, irritation mounting, in the end, impatience winning the night. "Oh, hell, condoms be damned. Come here."

The Health Center had a hard time giving those condoms away to the intended recipients. Sometimes you could see children blowing balloons of what were contrivances of frustration, discards of discontent.

3

When Mother and I came back home from church, the housemaids had set the table in the small dining room. My sisters, Juanita and Emiliana, came out of their bedrooms and after greetings were exchanged, we sat down to my favorite breakfast of eggs, sausages and fried rice and steaming coffee that scalded the tongue.

"*Señorito* Nene is home, too," said the housemaid as she served me more sausages.

Nene Escaño was more than a cousin; he was one of my closest friends. I had gone away to school, was now working in another city, had made acquaintances along the way, even called a few a friend, but I had not formed the kind of closeness with those others as I had with my cousins.

"I told him you had just arrived," the maid continued.

She was one of a number of household help who kept our lives dustless, spotless, precise, without chaos---the two housemaids who took care of the living room and bedrooms; the cook whose domain the family seldom visited, the houseboy who, contrary to his name, took care only of the grounds and the dogs, which were not allowed in the house; the laundrywoman who took out the laundry. It does not matter what you do, as long as you are the best in what you do, Mother would say when the laundrywoman brought back the laundry, smelling sweetly of sun, pressed to perfection.

"I'll go see him after breakfast," I told the maid. This one kept the dining rooms dusted and polished, and stood guard while we ate, serving food, drink and small talk. The marketplace, dark, dense, deep with chatter and gossip, droned with the latest each morning and the dining room maid and the cook came back from the baker's and the butcher's, laden with the morning bread, the day's meat and the bulletin of the day. Thus, we learned firsthand, without benefit of radio or newspaper, what was happening in town, who had arrived and who had left, heard the details of the latest scandal even before the concerned parties themselves were aware that their names were being smacked about in the marketplace like so many badminton shuttles.

It was a big meal, and I was bursting. I had almost forgotten the indulgence of these huge breakfasts. Now at work, I would just gulp down a cup of coffee and a roll and call that breakfast. I went to the window and looked out at the estuary at the back of our house. The river, swollen and full, rushing to meet the sea in one big hurry, had slowly eaten into our land, and was wider now than I remembered. The sea, too, had taken a large chunk of the shore. At high tide, the sea foam billowed and the bulging estuary churned, so full of activity that a couple of times it disgorged a stunned shark onto the sand. Later the townspeople knifed out every inch of its flesh, and hacked up all its bones down to the fins, which they believed were aphrodisiac, until not a trace of the carcass remained.

The dogs looked up at me and started barking. The houseboy was feeding them, big, black creatures I could not come near to because of my allergies. The houseboy was Mother's gofer. He went to town for this and that, took care of the dogs, maintained the grounds, and helped my sisters with the flowers. When summer was rife, he picked the fruits that were ripe for eating. After the fruits were gathered, he helped the wind shake the trees of brittle leaves, then swept them into great piles and burned them, and the breezes wafted the scent of burning leaves down the lane, inside the house, into the memory.

4

My mother, Mercedes Faelnar Aberásturi, was born in a town a few kilometers from Malitbog. She was a tall woman, slight of frame, very reserved in her manner and bearing, standing straight in appearance, straighter in principles.

Her father's sister, Agustina Faelnar Escaño, had married one of the province's richest men. One night, on a trip to Cebu City, there was a mutiny on the ship and her husband, Fernando Escaño, and some others were murdered. Agustina Faelnar Escaño, freshly widowed, with a dozen children in tow, came back from Manila to live in Malitbog, in their house that was called the *Casa*.

The *Casa* was more a mansion than a house, an immense structure with more than thirty rooms that occupied an entire block, the epitome of riches and elegance that would have been more at home in a big metropolis than in a sleepy town. It towered over and shadowed the more humble dwellings, and their less affluent owners, that made up the town. It had all the trappings of great wealth: polished hardwood floors, intricately designed furniture, iceboxes, imported crystal and silver and china, carpets and tapestries, embroidered linens, hot and cold water in bathrooms with porcelain tubs and lavatories. Parties for more than a hundred were held easily and often. In the dining rooms, overhead fans with cords that servants pulled back and forth cooled dinner guests. All this, the stream of cousins, nephews and nieces who came and stayed at any given time, as well as the care of the dozen children of Mother's aunt, required an army of servants to maintain.

Mother's family had some measure of wealth, owned some hectares of land. Then both my mother's parents died and her rich aunt Agustina took the orphans under her wing.

There in that great house my mother and her sister and brothers went to live with their aunt and cousins until Father came, saw Mother, married her and took her away.

-    -   -   -

My father was born in the town of Forua, deep in the Basque region of Spain. He was a big man, strongly built, with the typical broad frame of the Basques.

When young, while playing *jai alai*, that ball game that the Basques originated, a handball broke Father's nose, and gave his face a craggy, rugged look. He had intent gray eyes flecked with green and a quiet way of speaking that commanded obedience and belied a jocular streak. As far as I could remember, he had a full head of shiny silver hair and a bushy silver moustache. The first time we saw a movie with the director John Huston, we said, *Hey, there's Papa.*

Father's oldest brother Bruno Aberásturi came from Spain to Malitbog some fifteen years before Father. He was a captain of a *velero,* huge sailboats that plied these waters to collect copra and abaca, known as Manila hemp, the province's chief exports. Large ships that came from foreign shores used to dock on that same wharf from where we, much later, would dive, just a few meters from shore, but where the water was deep enough to carry those large foreign ships. Wagons piled high with bales of abaca and copra rolled out of the warehouse on rails, and workers filled the bowels of these ships with these most important exports of the province, and indeed of the country, that the family exported to England, Spain, the Netherlands, and the United States.

After several of these trips, one of the Escaño girls caught the eyes of my uncle Bruno. He wooed and wed fifteen-year-old Justina Escaño, the eldest daughter of my mother's aunt, Agustina. Subsequently, he brought her back with him to Forua, the Aberásturi hometown in Spain. Soon, the other Escaño children were going to school there, spending their vacations there, and making the town their base while they toured Europe.

Much later, Father had a cousin who also came to the Philippines from Spain. Victorino Aberásturi his name was. He worked on an Escaño ship and after a while married Pacita Escaño

Coromina, daughter of Mother's first cousin, Paz Escaño Coromina. One night in a raging storm, violent wind and waves mercilessly lashed and whipped the ship. The ship cracked and had to be abandoned. Workers on the ship knocked frantically on Victorino's cabin, trying to wake him up. It was a futile effort, however. The ship sank, bringing Victorino down with it to his deep-sea grave.

5

One of the sons of my mother's aunt was Lorenzo Escaño, Mother's first cousin who touched our lives the most. *Tio* Lorenzo went to Spain to get a degree in Commerce; since he was almost the same age as Father, they went to school together, first in Guernica where they studied at the Augustinian Friars School. At graduation, *Tio* Lorenzo received the highest grades the school had ever bestowed on a student, a scholastic record not topped for quite some time. From there, he and Father both went to Eton, in England, along the way forging a friendship that would last their lifetimes.

At Eton they absorbed and polished their English, and both got high grades. Then *Tio* Lorenzo discovered the horse races. After that, he spent his time trying to figure out which horse was going to win and his grades took a nosedive. Just when he had worked out a system of predicting the winners in the races (so he said), his mother, Agustina, ordered him to come home to manage the family business. When he objected, his mother threatened to cut off his allowance, which forced him to return.

When he arrived in Malitbog, their family business, the *Hijos de Fernando Escaño,* which at that time was engaged in shipping and the export of abaca, was in disarray. When *Tio* Lorenzo took over its management, he realized that his mother did not just use the state of the family business as a ruse to bring him back home; the business was really on the brink of bankruptcy. *Tio* Lorenzo wrote Father to come and help him bring order to the business in chaos, help him put the business to right. Father left Spain to work with *Tio* Lorenzo managing the business, stayed in one of the more than thirty rooms in the *Casa,* and there saw Mother.

My mother's aunt liked to organize dances and very often held such affairs in the spacious living room of the *Casa.* Mother was a good dancer, although most of the time, she just danced with her own cousins.

Father did not know how to dance, except the jota, the Basque folk dance, so he just stayed in the background, observing the many young ladies who lived in the *Casa*---my mother, her sister, her first cousins---and the inevitable guests. Ultimately, he fixed his gaze on Mother. He married her, and built her a house, a small one at first, then one a little bigger and, finally, that big house.

-    -   -   -

My parents' first child was a boy who died in infancy. After him came my sisters, Cristina, Juanita, Emiliana, and Clotilde, four girls in a row, and then my brother Ramon was born. There was much jubilation when he arrived, a long-awaited boy beautiful to behold. He was baptized in a grand and princely fashion, one of the very few times in their lives my parents came out of their simple, circumspect way of living to celebrate the coming of a long-awaited son. A cow and various livestock were slaughtered for the occasion, bags of coins were tossed in the air when the baptismal party came out of the church, and a feast was shared not only by the family, but by the townspeople as well.

Along the way, so as not to spend money on clothes, Mother, that wellspring of frugality, did not discourage it when, doting on such an adorable brother, my sisters dressed him in their hand-me-downs, so that on top of the girl-clothes, my brother also got my sisters' mannerisms. Father did not let this pass. When my brother walked and talked and acted like my sisters, Father, thirsting for a *boy* boy, smacked my brother's behind with his large hand. Those fingers big as cigars cuffed away the feminine mannerisms, shaping a son much like himself, straight, upright and principled, attributes which I, later indulged by a father secretly pleased with a son who was more a handful than he ever hoped for, did not appreciate then, when all my cares, it seemed, centered on the everyday concerns of an indulged youth.

The excitement of the birth of a boy had waned when I arrived. Nothing special celebrated my coming. No festivities were planned for my baptism; nobody was invited; nobody came. When they brought me to church, Mother asked the priest how much she had to pay for the baptismal service.

"Five or ten, depending," the priest answered.

"Depending on what, Father?" Mother asked cautiously.

"For five, you don't get church bells," he explained.

"Oh, never mind the church bells, Father," said Mother. It was one thing to give to the church, which she did, profusely and often; it was another to needlessly proclaim attention to oneself, and pay for it, too. However, the boys up on the church steeple who were charged with ringing the bells were not advised of this discounted arrangement. In the middle of the baptismal rites, the bells tolled happily.

"Father," Mother warned grimly, "I am not paying for bells."

"Never mind, then," said the good priest, quite amused. "The bells are on me."

And so my soul was ushered into the Church, amidst the tintinnabulation of bargain bells.

6

When Cristina was eleven and Juanita nine, Father brought them to Spain to study. Father's hometown, Forua, was a ten-minute walk from the town of Guernica, and an hour's drive from Bilbao, the capital of the Basque province of Vizcaya. Father decided that now was a good time for his daughters to get to know his family and to become acquainted with the land he was born and grew up in. Father's older brother, *Tio* Raimundo, was the parish priest of Larrauri, a small village about an hour's drive from Forua. His two older sisters, *Tia* Margarita and *Tia* Josefa, kept house for *Tio* Raimundo in the vicarage and Father figured that living with them would be a good influence on his daughters.

Nineteen thirty-one was not the best year to bring two young girls to Spain to study in a religious boarding school, however. The Spanish monarchy had just been deposed and a Republican government installed. King Alfonso XIII went into exile and the new government had socialists and anarchists in its ministries who were anti-Catholic and opposed religious instruction. The government started closing down religious schools.

For safety, *Tio* Raimundo enrolled Cristina and Juanita in a local orphanage run by the sisters of Saint Joseph, where he was the chaplain and confessor. After about two years, noting that the school did not provide much in the area of real education in literature and the classics, *Tio* Raimundo decided it was safe enough to enroll his nieces in a real boarding school. He chose Berriz, an exclusive school for girls run by the Mercedarian Sisters, up in the mountains, about a two-hour drive from Larrauri.

To circumvent the law against religious-run schools, the Mother Superior transferred the title of ownership of the school to a lay Catholic relative and the school reopened. The nuns involved with teaching and running the school had to discard their habits.

Now they wore civilian suits and dresses and were addressed as *Señoritas* instead of *Sisters*.

The Spanish Civil War broke out during the summer vacation of 1936 and lasted for three years. On July 16, there was an uprising by the military, called the Nationalists, who wanted to take over the Republican government. Everybody, including the military, thought it would be an easy matter to oust the Republicans; *Tio* Raimundo even thought that Cristina and Juanita could go back to school when school opened in the first week of October.

In Larrauri, Cristina and Juanita were spending their summer vacation in the vicarage with *Tio* Raimundo, *Tia* Margarita and *Tia* Josefa. The Civil War was already raging across Spain, although they at Larrauri were hardly aware of it yet. By August, *Tio* Raimundo received notice from the Mother Superior that the school in Berriz would be closed until the hostilities ended and to wait for further notice. Thus their vacation, quite ordinary at this time, was extended indefinitely.

An unusual event that Juanita remembered was the arrival of a lady with four children. She came to Larrauri to seek refuge from the bombings which had become a regular event in Bilbao. That was when they at Larrauri realized that the war had inched nearer to where they were. Eventually, even Larrauri would not be safe anymore. When the first planes went over Larrauri, Juanita was downstairs with Maria, an old lady who was staying in the apartment below; she was peeling some potatoes and a basket of vegetables stood beside her. When she heard the planes coming down low, Maria hid her head in the basket, which made Juanita burst out laughing. The planes just passed over, and when Maria saw Juanita laughing, she nicknamed her *Juanita, La Poca Pena* (Juanita, The Sorrowless).

They spent Christmas at Larrauri that year, uneventful to the girls but for the visit of Ciriaco, a cousin, a tall, good-looking man in his middle twenties. He had been fighting at the front and was given a short leave to spend Christmas with his family in Bilbao. On his way, he decided to stop and pay his respects to *Tio* Raimundo. When *Tio* Raimundo asked him how it felt to fire a gun aimed at a living person, he said that at the beginning he always pointed his gun high to make sure he did not hit anyone, but then, the grim realities of civil war set in. After he saw his own buddies falling down and dying, and faced with the possibility that the next body to fall could be his own, he made sure that his bullets hit their target.

-    -   -   -

Meanwhile, Italians and Germans started to arrive in Morocco and the Balearic Islands, taking a large part in the military operations of the rebel Nationalists. Germany had a great interest in the insurgents' victory: with the Nationalists in power, Germany could use the Balearic Islands to implement Hitler's grandiose plan to develop sea power in the Mediterranean; the large German population in Barcelona could be useful for political and military espionage, and Morocco was of great interest---from Morocco, Germany could secure a foothold on Northern Africa.

For Italy, with the Nationalists in power, she could establish bases in Spain in the event of war with France.

The League of Nations, fearful that foreign involvement in the Spanish Civil War---Italy and Germany aiding the cause of the Nationalist rebels of Generalissimo Francisco Franco---*El Caudillo*, The Leader, as he was called, and the Soviet Union supporting the Republicans, the duly elected government of Spain---would drag Europe into a major European conflagration, formed the Non-Intervention Committee in the summer of 1936, with Great Britain and France spearheading the plan. The meeting was attended by representatives of all European countries, except Switzerland, which had always taken the standpoint of neutrality. Twenty-seven countries signed the Agreement, including Germany, Italy, the Soviet Union and Portugal.

His signature on the Agreement did not stop Mussolini from continuing his support to Franco, however; Italy signed a secret treaty with the Nationalists. In exchange for military aid, the Nationalists would allow Italy to establish bases in Spain. During the first months of the Agreement, Italy sent military aid to Spain: Italian aircraft, thousands of tons of bombs, hundreds of cannons and mortars, machine guns, and motor vehicles. Most of the arms in the Nationalist rebels' possession originated from Italy. Hitler as well continued to send aid to Franco, in violation of the Non-Intervention Pact, of which he was one of the signatories. He sent hundreds of airplanes and thousands of soldiers; he sent transport planes to Morocco to aid Franco in airlifting troops and hundreds of tons of war material to Spain. Without these planes, it would have taken Franco many months, instead of just two, to transport all this war material from Africa to Spain.

- - - -

The first planes that passed over Larrauri did not drop any bombs, but they came down very low and sent people scrambling out of their houses. *Tio* Raimundo knew that the next contingent of planes would not be as harmless; he instructed his parishioners to run as fast as they could to the relative safety of the stone-walled bell tower the next time they hear the drone of oncoming planes. True enough, the next time they came, they dropped bombs on the recreation hall of the orphanage, killing one girl and wounding many others. There were other sporadic bombings after that, and people started leaving town to look for places they thought safer.

Down in the valley, further down from the vicarage, was a farmhouse owned by people who used to supply *Tio* Raimundo with goat cheese. *Tio* Raimundo decided that in the meantime, it would be safer to seek refuge there. The valley was isolated, was on lower ground, and there were the mountains on both sides to protect it. Cristina and Juanita heard that the owner of the farmhouse had a son who did not want to fight for the government forces and so hid in their attic. The farmhouse was so well sheltered that the girls never even saw him, even though they knew that he was there.

One day, the daughter of the owner of the farmhouse came home from fetching water. *Tio* Raimundo saw her carrying the jug of water, and a spent shell about a foot and half long and ten inches in diameter. She was just an unschooled girl; she did not know that the shell might burst any minute. In very casual tones so as not to scare the girl, *Tio* Raimundo told her to take the shell, very slowly, as far away from the house as possible. Only later did the poor girl know how close she was to being blown out of this world.

But the country was at war and there was no safe haven.

Juanita was enjoying the afternoon under a grape vine which was starting to put out buds when she heard a whizzing sound overhead. A cannon shell followed, tumbling and doing cartwheels and landed about twenty feet away. She was shocked and dumbfounded, stunned motionless; she held her breath and waited for the explosion. This was one big bomb, almost two feet long, similar to the one the girl had brought home. If it exploded, "I wouldn't be here to tell this story." But it did not, bringing Juanita back to the present. She raced to *Tio* Raimundo. He decided there was no place safe enough; they might as well just go back to the vicarage. They bundled their belongings and trudged back home.

It was Larrauri in chaos that met them, however. They did not even have a chance to go up to the vicarage.

Officers of the Falange, the fascist political group that served Franco, were knocking on every door, telling everyone to get out of town. The place was not safe; gunboats from the other side of the mountain on the shore along Baquio were shelling government forces atop the other mountain and shells were raining about.

Soon, they were the only ones left in the area. *Tio* Raimundo wanted to get back to the vicarage to get some of their belongings but was stopped by a Falange officer. "You cannot go back there," the officer warned *Tio* Raimundo, "and there is no time to lose. You must get away from here. You have to hurry; run to the highway now." He then gave *Tio* Raimundo instructions. "Listen for the shells; first you will hear a boom. If a whistling sound follows, fall on the ground immediately. It means a shell is coming your way. If you don't hear the whistling sound, continue running. But hurry, hurry!"

Off they went, *Tio* Raimundo and his two sisters, well over their sixties, and their two teenaged nieces, running down the hill towards the main highway, falling down on their faces every time the dreaded sound whistled over their heads! Juanita was not *Juanita, la poca pena* anymore; she was just a scared little girl, running fast and as far away from the raining shells.

Once again, chaos met them when they finally arrived on the highway. Soldiers were everywhere, in different uniforms, speaking different languages. People were crowding about, lost like everyone else, not knowing what to do or where to go. Fear was palpable in the air. Finally, an officer approached *Tio* Raimundo and in broken Spanish asked him where they were going.

Tio Raimundo said he wanted to go to Forua but there was no transportation. "It's getting dark and we have no place to spend the night."

Tio Raimundo was in his black soutane; the officer was Italian, and most probably a Catholic. He made signs for them to follow him. They came to a barn, empty of animals but with plenty of baled hay. It turned out that the officer's unit was using the barn as their communication center. Big black boxes entangled with wires, which looked like radio equipment, were on tables.

"You could stay the night here, but you will have to leave first thing tomorrow, it's not safe for you here." The officer looked over at the hay. "You could sleep there." He gave them bread and cheese. "I'm sure you're hungry."

Tio Raimundo thanked him. Cristina recalled that the bread and cheese were delicious and the hay was most comfortable. They fell asleep immediately.

The next day, the officer directed them to a bus that was leaving for Bermeo. Bermeo was not their destination, but it was on the way to Forua, and it was better than staying another night in the barn. In Bermeo, they were given a room to stay for the rest of the day and night. Here all spoke Spanish and there were no officers around, which made them a little less lost. The next day, they left for Forua.

In Forua, *Tia* Josefa always had beddings, pillows and towels, as well as kitchen and dining utensils, kept for the times they stayed there during vacation. As for clothing, however, there was nothing.

"Not to worry," *Tia* Josefa reassured them, "we shall go to Guernica." They usually walked the ten-minute distance to

Guernica to shop for their more important needs. She did not realize that just a week before, the German Condor Legion razed Guernica to the ground, and all stores had been closed.

-     -   -   -

Guernica, the Luftwaffe's dry run for World War II. With a vastly inferior air force, Generalissimo Francisco Franco sought the aid of Germany; in July Hitler received the appeal for help. Hitler immediately convened his ministers and a plan of military support was formed. Hitler ordered the formation of the Condor Legion, a force of some 100 aircraft and almost 12,000 men.

Germany was eager to use Spain in testing new weapons and methods of warfare, and Guernica, especially, for its emerging Luftwaffe. On the national level, an attack on Guernica would demonstrate to the Republicans---Madrid, Barcelona, Valencia and Basque Bilbao---the military superiority of the Nationalists. The Republican army was composed more of idealists than of military-trained men. Franco, on the other hand, was born into a military family, went to school at the Toledo Infantry Academy, and served as director of the General Military Academy of Zaragoza, a college for Army cadets. He had already established a reputation for cruelty, having brutally crushed the uprising in Spanish Morocco, and quelled the strike of coal miners in Asturias. On the international viewpoint, an attack on Guernica would give Western Europe a glimpse of the horrible aftermath of an attack launched on a defenseless town.

Hitler's major contribution to the Spanish Civil War was the German Condor Legion under the command of Lieutenant Colonel Wolfram von Richthofen. Richthofen chose Guernica: small town, defenseless, with no apparent means of retaliation. Besides which the Basques, intensely proud and self-sufficient, had long posed a problem, with their protracted demands for autonomy and independence.

The *Murder of Guernica,* the locals called that bloody Monday of April in 1937, a market day when farmers from all around the countryside went to Guernica to sell their produce, buy their weekly provisions, and end up in the evening with a *romeria,* public dancing in the town plaza, before heading back home.

Instead of the merry-making, that day ended in a terrible slaughter of men, women, children and animals.

The planes came in the middle of the afternoon, dropping thousands of kilos of bombs on the unsuspecting town, flying so low that the German pilots could be seen laughing as they strafed women and children diving into what they thought was the relative safety of ditches along the road. But the German pilots machine-gunned everything they set their eyes on, even herds of cattle along the roads. People scampering for shelter were sprayed with pieces of bodies of animal. Black smoke darkened the skies. Panic was everywhere, fanned by the overpowering heat from the enormous conflagration.

Guernica burned for three days. This would go down in history as the first aerial mass terror bombing of civilians.

Guernica was the combat debut of the *Stuka* dive bombers, flown by Germany's Condor Legion, with their screaming sirens, followed by the explosion of their bombs that sent terror in the hearts of the populace. Their infamous *Jericho Trumpet*, wailing air sirens, became the propaganda symbol of German air power in the horrifying days to come.

By the time the German Condor Legion left, Guernica was in ruins--1654 were dead and 889 wounded. There was an international condemnation. Western Europe, and the world, were outraged and denounced Germany for her involvement. The Basque painter Pablo Picasso painted his celebrated *Guernica,* which dramatized the destruction of the Basque village, bringing Guernica and the Spanish Civil War to the attention of the world.

The International Brigades, made up of foreign volunteers from more than fifty countries, flocked to Spain to help fight against Franco's Fascist forces.

World press coverage was unparalleled. Celebrated authors, like Ernest Hemingway and George Orwell, covered the war. Hemingway would later base his book *For Whom the Bell Tolls* on his experience in Spain, and the British writer George Orwell wrote *Homage to Catalonia*, documenting the time he spent in the Spanish Civil War.

Although every member nation of the Non-Intervention Pact was aware that Germany and Italy were violating the Agreement and sending aid to Franco, no aid was given to the Republicans, who were begging France and Britain to sell them arms.

Behind the wall of neutrality and the Non-Intervention Agreement, England and France watched the annihilation of Guernica and its civilian population. Guernica was, in fact, a major factor in Neville Chamberlain's Policy of Appeasement. An English countryside being razed down once again by Germany's dive bombers was a picture too horrible for Chamberlain to contemplate.

Flush with his accomplishment in Spain, Hitler demanded that the Czechs return to Germany the Sudetenland, which was stripped from Germany in the Treaty of Versailles after World War I. Although France had treaty commitments to the Czechs, French Prime Minister Daladier joined Britain's Chamberlain in appeasing Hitler, and urged the Czech Government "to agree, and agree promptly," to Hitler's demand.

Thus, on the eve of the Second World War, Europe stood by while Hitler "tested the waters" in Spain, sowed the seeds of territorial aggression and *Lebensraum* in Europe, as Germany annexed the Sudetenland, marched with impunity into Austria, entered Prague and occupied the entire country without much protest from other Western powers. With the invasion of Poland in September of 1939, Germany goose-stepped into the Second World War and plunged the world into the deadliest conflict in human history.

7

At home, Father was getting news of the uprising on his radio, but he was not yet very alarmed: nobody thought the war was going to last long and not everyone was aware how serious the uprising had become. Mother was beside herself with worry, however, and kept urging Father to get my sisters out. After a few months and the uprising did not show signs of abating, Father started having serious misgivings himself. He contacted the US Consulate in Cebu. By March of 1937, the State Department in Washington, DC sent a telegram to the US Consul in Bilbao, informing him of Father's intention to go to Spain to get his daughters out. The US Consul issued a certificate that "Dionisio Aberásturi is the father of Cristina and Juana Aberásturi, citizens of the Philippine Islands under the sovereignty of the United States of America," entreating the Military and Civilian authorities to give all necessary facilities to Father to accomplish the purpose of his trip. In May, Father boarded a ship for France; because of the situation in Spain, the US Consul to Spain had taken temporary residence in St. Jean de Luz. The US Consul gave Father instructions on how to get my sisters out of Spain.

A female officer of the Falange went to Forua to inform *Tio* Raimundo that Father was in France waiting to take Cristina and Juanita out. "All formalities had already been approved," she told *Tio* Raimundo. "However, being a Spaniard, your brother cannot enter Spain, otherwise, he might not be allowed to come out."

"I cannot even talk to my brother?"

"I'm sorry but you will not be allowed," the Falange officer said. The officer saw the sorrow on Tio Raimundo's face. "I understand how you feel, but they will not allow you to talk to him. Maybe five minutes, definitely no more than that."

"What am I allowed to do?" asked *Tio* Raimundo.

"Your brother must go to Hendaye, the French side of the frontier. You take the girls to Irun, which is on the Spanish side of the frontier. Then they can just cross the border to Hendaye."

Tio Raimundo said he would rather not go. It would be too painful not to spend even just an hour with his youngest brother. He sent a cousin instead, to take Cristina and Juanita to the frontier.

Father was waiting for them in Hendaye. In Irun, on the Spanish side of the frontier, Father saw his two daughters, carrying with them a small bundle. They ran across the border to where Father was waiting. He had not seen them in six years! He held on to them, then he embraced his cousin. They exchanged a few words, then a silent wave. Less than five minutes, that was all it took, that was all they were allowed.

The girls had carried with them a small bag, filling it with only a very few articles of clothing, actually, the only things they owned, since they were not allowed to return to their house in Larrauri to retrieve their other possessions. But they filled the bag with a dozen apples from their orchard. That night in their hotel, Cristina opened the bag.

"Look, Papa," said Cristina, as the delicious aroma of apples filled the room.

"Apples?" said Father. He looked almost stunned.

This was worth more than all the satisfaction they would have gotten had they been allowed to take out their other belongings, watching the pleasure on Father's face, listening to the crunch of the apple as he bit into it. "I know where you picked this one," he said, happily describing the part of their orchard where the largest and plumpest apples grew.

Father spent the next day arranging their passage for home. The earliest departure date he could get was in two weeks. This gave them time to do a little sightseeing. They went to Biarritz to visit Father's friend, a man named Cincunegui. They stayed in Biarritz for two days. Juanita remembered that they went to a "high class beach" with Cincunegui's daughters, but they stayed in a second-class hotel. From Biarritz, they went to Paris, and then to Lourdes. In Lourdes, they witnessed a candle-lit evening procession, a stirring experience, with every devotee singing the Immaculate Mother song in his own language, and then everyone joining in singing the Ave Maria. "It was very moving."

From there they went to Rome, and visited the Catacombs. Then on to Naples, where they went up Mount Vesuvius and watched the lava pouring down. They brought home souvenirs of coins dipped in lava and dried, with the coins imbedded in them. They stayed in Venice while they waited for their departure date. They had more fun in Venice. Father had a great sense of adventure, preferring a Venetian exploration on foot rather than on a gondola, which they tried only a couple of times. Then it was time to go home.

They sailed for Hong Kong from Trieste on the Italian ocean liner Lloyd Triestino, "where we stayed in second class," Juanita recalled. From Hong Kong they sailed for Manila on the Empress of Japan, "still in second class." But they were in good company; Cristina remembered that at their table in the dining room was Camilo Osias, the distinguished author "who spoke very good Spanish."

This was the last time Father went back to Spain.

-    -   -   -

They were strangers to me when they arrived, two sisters I had not seen before, having left before I was born, some dozen years older than I. I remember them being very thin, like Mother. Or maybe it was the war that made them so.

Since they spoke only Spanish, Father sent them to Saint Catherine's School in Carcar, run by Belgian sisters, situated outside the city of Cebu, to learn English. There they stayed until they were proficient in that language.

The city of Cebu is the largest city in the southern part of the Philippines. It is the center of commerce, industry and education; some of the oldest and best schools in the country are located in that city, and families from neighboring provinces send their children to the Catholic schools there mostly run by priests and nuns.

At this time, my sisters Emiliana and Clotilde were already boarders at the *Colegio de la Inmaculada Concepcion* in Cebu, a girls' school run by the Sisters of Mercy. My cousins sent their daughters there at a very young age to start school. Here they lived until they finished school, going back home to Malitbog only on vacations, living with the nuns longer than they did with their parents. Here Father transferred Juanita from the school in Carcar.

When Emiling Aberásturi Gonzalez, daughter of Father's brother, Bruno, learned that Father was transferring my sisters from Carcar, she asked if Cristina could live in their house while she was in Cebu. Emiling had a daughter, Carmen, who was the same age as Cristina. In those days, a young girl was not allowed to go out without a chaperone, and Cristina and Carmen could chaperone each other. As this would be one less worry for Father, he agreed, and Cristina lived with Emiling in Cebu while she studied painting and music.

8

After breakfast, I put on my shorts and prepared to go out. It was my first day home, a swim in the sea was in order. I grabbed a towel and went to visit Nene Escaño at the villa. I drove the jeep well into the villa's grounds, past the palm trees that lined the driveway, scraggly remnants of orchids clinging to their trunks.

Tio Agustin Escaño, one of Mother's first cousins, built this villa at the end of town when he got married, and named it *Villa Margarita* after his wife. It was a showcase of a house, sitting on several hectares of land, with a formal garden that used to be tended by a Japanese gardener.

It looked a bit dilapidated now. The vibrant colors of long ago had turned a nondescript gray. Paint peelrd off the walls. The flowering vines that used to curl up the curlicues on the wrought metal railings on the windows safeguarding the first floor rooms now looked withered and tired. On the second floor, the front bedroom verandas overlooking the gardens did not look safe enough to linger on. But I did not like it any the less for that. Like a beloved friend who had grown grayer, its drab shell could not lessen the affection I felt for it, this house that I always found more elegant than even the *Casa*.

I first got drunk here when I was eleven. We were celebrating Juanita's birthday and as usual, we were all in attendance: cousins, friends, even children of friends who came to Malitbog at the advent of the war to avoid the Japanese in Cebu. "All right," said Raul Cruz, son of one of Father's friends who evacuated to Malitbog. "Come you young men," he announced as he gathered us children together. "Let's have a contest here. All right, we have Paquito here." He named some other cousins who had crowded around him. "We have Txomin here. Let's see who of you young men can drink up the most."

He, and some others, had concocted a potion they called a cocktail, made of *tuba*, the fermented coconut drink, which they mixed with lemon juice, sugar and who knew what else.

I took the drink from Raul's hand, and tossed it down in one hard swallow. The drink gurgled down my throat, protesting the fast gulp, a stranger to my uninitiated throat. I went into a paroxysm of coughing and the drink sprayed out of my mouth. I could not stop coughing and Raul thumped my back. I harrumphed a few times to clear the liquid from my throat. "Oh, Jeez, what the heck was that?" I sputtered, coughing some more.

Raul gave my back another thump as I took deep breaths to clear my breathing passages.

"You okay now?" asked Raul when I appeared more calm.

"Guess so."

"He's good, he's good," announced Raul, "and ready for another one!"

It was a disgusting brew, one I would not even have taken a sniff of at any other time. There are firsts in one's young life, however, when one cannot call on experience for help. I do not remember how many more glasses they foisted on me; in fact I do not remember much after the first one. My sisters were at the other parts of the house and were not aware of the foolishness Raul had contrived. Juanita remembered that we were walking home, they were puzzled at the way I was weaving my way through the street. Raul took her aside.

"He's a bit plastered," he said.

"A bit plastered?" Juanita said. "Why, he can hardly walk. Whatever did you do?"

"We gave him some things to drink, but he'll be okay," he said. "Just be sure you get him to bed immediately when you get home. Be sure *Tia* Merced does not see him."

Sure enough, Mother was the one who opened the door and there we were. There I was, the world revolving around me, feeling all of my insides coming out. "Ach," the sound came from within me, and out flew the brew that they called a cocktail, straight into the front of Mother's dress.

My sisters said later that Mother was so angry she started beating my butt with her hand. All the commotion drew Father from his room.

"What's happening here?" Father asked. My sisters explained to him what Raul did. "Ced," Father said, calm and patient, as he always was, composed and unruffled even in the face of distress.

"Ced," he said, trying to cool Mother down. Most everyone cut short Mother's name, Mercedes, to Merced, and those close to her cut it even shorter, to Ced. "He is too intoxicated to understand what's happening. Leave him alone tonight; you can do this tomorrow."

"Tomorrow when I'm not angry anymore?" fumed Mother, still beating my behind with her hand, "no, he's going to get it well and good tonight."

This was my initiation into the Drinkers' Club, whose members, mostly uncles and cousins, took great amusement in the way I, so young and small, handled my drink, at least until I disgorged it all on Mother. Although this was the first time I had a drink and did not have one again for the next four years or so, I was now a bona fide member of this distinguished club, with the distinction of being the youngest.

I did much justice to the responsibilities of this membership that over the years my reputation crossed the seas. When my brother Ramon became engaged to a daughter of one of the prominent families of a neighboring island, her aunt, who knew my sister, warned: "Cristina has two brothers. Be sure Consuelo is not marrying the one who drinks a lot."

This incident must have left a lasting impression on me: that I could drink, but I must know how to carry it. Through the years I have learned to hold my drink and never threw up again.

-    -   -   -

I parked the jeep under a tree at the side of the villa, pocketed the keys, and walked over to the entrance of the house. The air was redolent with the earthy smells of summer and bees droned everywhere. The terrace floor was strewn with petals; I tried not to step on them as I lit a cigarette. I snapped the lighter close on the flame fluttering in the breeze and took a deep, satisfying drag as I looked around. Wisteria vines clung to columns that supported the second-story balcony. Blue-violet petals clustered copiously among the leaves; huge, varicosey veins ran through the gray vines as thick as arms. I did not even know that wisteria grew in the tropics, but here they were, had been here ever since I could remember. A breeze blew petals off the stems and they came twirling down languidly, resting on my shoulders as I stood on their way. Yesterday's petals, dusty blue now, mingled with the new bright violet ones and covered the two benches flanking the terrace. The *santol* trees at the sides of the house towered high against the sky, shading the house. Little green fruits clung to their branches. In a short time, they would ripen into sweet, yellow fruits to be harvested and sent to houses of relatives.

The huge door was open as it often was.

Inside, large bedrooms occupied both sides of the first level. In the center, a great staircase winged up the second story. I took the stairs two steps at a time to the second floor. Here were rooms just as large: a foyer, a dining room, a library, a formal sitting room, bedrooms with their own balconies, all with frescoed ceilings, frieze covered walls, frescoes that *Tio* Agustin himself had painted. Wide verandas ran on both sides of the house and poured light into the rooms.

On black, moonless nights or when a storm threatened outside, nephews and nieces often gathered here and with the wind moaning through the trees, played Spirit of the Glass and scared themselves to delicious death by telling tall ghost stories.

-    -   -   -

Tio Agustin, like his younger brother, *Tio* Lorenzo, studied in London. A gentle man and a gentleman, he was the artist in a family of lovers of the arts. After London, he went to Italy to study painting and spent vacations in Spain. He was an accomplished musician and an excellent painter, was well read and widely traveled.

Margarita Javier and her sister, Maria Javier, were spending the summer at the convent where their brother, the parish priest of the town, lived. There, *Tio* Agustin first saw *Tia* Margarita. A romantic at heart, he would serenade her at the convent, bringing with him an entire band, and a ladder, which he would prop up outside her bedroom window. He would climb up the ladder and court her through the window while the band played below. He married her, built a villa at the end of town, and named it Villa Margarita.

After they married, they traveled abroad and stocked the villa with treasures they brought back---crate after crate of works of art, rare coins, exquisite sets of vases, lamps with stands of marble figures and women in Grecian robes, alabaster statues, old books and manuscripts with which they filled their library. When little, I would visit the library with my father and wide-eyed, listen to the bear footstool as it played music when someone sat on it. I would imagine all sorts of treasure it hoarded, a cache not unlike that of the bearded, black-caped, ghost-like figure from *Monte Cristo*.

And clocks. *Tio* Agustin had many and he wound them every day of his life so that for some time after he died, the clocks still chimed the hour. Then of course they realized that *Tio* Agustin was not there anymore to wind them to life and their chimes died with him.

A most devoted husband, *Tio* Agustin indulged *Tia* Margarita at every turn, and catered to her every wish. *Tia* Margarita just had to say the word and the word was done. "Ting," she would say to *Tio* Agustin, "I think the drapes need changing." Or, "We need a good gardener for the gardens." Or, "I don't think we are ever going to have children. Why don't we just adopt Emit?" And lo and behold, the drapes were changed, a Japanese gardener was hired, and Emit was adopted.

His real name was Emeterio Javier. He was *Tia* Margarita's nephew, one of the sons of her brother, *Señor* Emilio Javier. *Señor* Emilio and his wife supervised *Tio* Agustin's huge coconut and rice plantation a few kilometers outside of Malitbog. Since they had other children, and knowing that Emit would have a much better life with *Tio* Agustin and *Tia* Margarita, they agreed when the adoption was proposed, and Emit was adopted.

Tio Agustin and *Tia* Margarita raised Emit as a true son of the house, pampered and catered to, doted on by the gentle *Tio* Agustin and indulged in by the indulged *Tia* Margarita.

They sent him to the best schools in Manila, first to San Beda, where, after a short stint, the Benedictine Fathers asked him to leave for conduct unbecoming a San Bedan. Then he went to the *Colegio de* San Juan *de* Letran. Here, the Dominican priests were more patient and forgiving, and he stayed.

While Emit was still quite young, *Tio* Agustin and *Tia* Margarita decided to go on a European tour and took Emit with them, crossing the ocean in a luxury liner. When the ship had shows of women cavorting on stage, *Tia* Margarita covered Emit's eyes with her fan. "Don't look, don't look," she cautioned him. Then Emit got sick. A doctor was summoned, and he pronounced the affliction The Sickness From Women.

Tia Margarita was livid. "How could that be, how could that be?" she ranted. This was the boy, after all, on whom they spent so much love and effort, not to mention money, protecting. "He's so young, he's never allowed to look at, much less *be* with, a woman, these foreign doctors don't know what they're talking about," she raved. "Let's get a second opinion."

But a second, or a twentieth, could not alleviate *Tia* Margarita's wrath. Another foreign doctor was summoned, the same condition was pronounced. In a rage, she banged and banged her head against the wall. This was a habit shared with other members of her family, punishing a blameless wall with their heads when they were mad or angered or crossed.

-    -   -   -

When your name was Escaño, and you had the good looks and the money that came with it, the women were never far behind. When Emit saw a girl he fancied, he and another cousin, Otic Escaño, the son of *Tio* Agustin's brother, *Tio* Nemesio Escaño, would go to the girl's parents and ask for her hand in marriage. Emit would say, "My parents are out of the country," or some other excuse the two cousins had gleefully devised, "but my father sent his brother's son, Otic Escaño, to take his place, to ask for your daughter's hand in marriage." Never mind that the cousin looked suspiciously too young to stand in the parents' stead. Since it was not every day that an Escaño asked for the hand of the daughter of the house in marriage, the suit was always accepted. When he asked. Sometimes, he just took.

After the betrothal, the girl's parents allowed Emit certain liberties betrothed couples were allowed. Further liberties, though not explicitly given, were certainly taken, until too much familiarity bred ennui and some other things, and then another girl caught his roving eye. Otic Escaño would again act in behalf of Emit's parents, whose whereabouts would again be fabricated by the two cousins, and the same courting rituals would take place over again. Later, young men and women popped up in Emit's life, claiming their mothers told them that their father was Emeterio Escaño. He would dig into his memory and match women he remembered with places he had been to, and say, *yes, maybe, yes, that's possible.*

-    -   -   -

Once when in Manila, Emit met Dolores Rusca. He married her and brought her back with him to live in the villa with *Tio* Agustin. She was an exquisite, petite, especially sweet woman whom they called Lolita.

Neither Lolita, nor marriage, nor even the two handsome, strapping sons that Lolita gave him, ever obstructed Emit's view of fields of consenting females, which made more claimants to *Tio* Agustin's fortune an alarming possibility.

Tio Agustin took walks most afternoons and when he did, he would pass by our house at the other end of town and spend a few minutes with my parents.

One day, he said he had instituted proceedings to adopt Emit's two legitimate sons, Agustin Junior, who was called Nene, and Ramon, "I worry that these two boys might find themselves in the street when I'm gone," *Tio* Agustin said to my parents. This adoption would make them legal heirs of *Tio* Agustin, and so would give them equal rights and share when *Tio* Agustin's estate passed into inheritance.

Emit's business took him out of the villa most of the time, Lolita was just too fragile when she was there, so that even before she disappeared, the care of her two sons fell into the hands of *Tio* Agustin, hands that were just as gentle. He spoiled Nene and Ramon just as he and *Tia* Margarita spoiled Emit.

It was a good life Lolita lived in the villa, a life of ease, prestige and luxury, and whatever shortcomings Emit had, *Tio* Agustin compensated for, in countless ways. But would that Someone had written a softer ending to her sad story!

9

I went straight to Nene's bedroom. He was sitting on his bed, fiddling with a rifle. He owned quite a few firearms and was often tinkering with one or the other. Among his cache was a Colt 45, a 30-caliber M-1 carbine, a shotgun; a Smith and Wesson, "jet center fire magnum," he later introduced it to me. And now this rifle, which I had not seen before.

"Hey, Bud, look at this," he said without any overture. Friends more than cousins since we were children, our relationship had reached a level where none was needed. I took a last draw on my cigarette, and crushed it on an ashtray on his bedside table before I went over to examine his new acquisition.

"Yes," he said proudly, "22-caliber, lever action."

They had named him Agustin Escaño, Junior, after *Tio* Agustin, but he was Emit's offspring through and through. He was as conversant with guns, as good-looking, and was as appealing to women as Emit was before him, leading to a tumultuous relationship with his girlfriend, Felicing. They went to school in Cebu and when they quarreled, which was often, he would appear outside her classroom intoxicated, and would start a commotion to make her come out. When she did, he would slash his middle with a knife and carry on and cry and bleed, knowing that with the blood and the tears came her forgiveness.

Once, he cut his stomach deeper than usual.

"Oh, Jeez, Buddy, what did you do here?" I looked at the gaping wound on his middle, oozing with blood, and I almost fainted. Blood is a stranger I refuse to deal with. I looked away and gulped in as much air as I could to steady myself. There was just too much blood and we had to take him to my sister Juanita. Nothing fazed Juanita. She rolled a wad of cotton around a stick, dipped it in iodine, and rubbed and poked and jabbed the dripping stick into the yawning wound.

Nene caught his breath, wincing. "Ouch."

"Ouch?" Juanita said, "a big fearless fellow like you?" She changed wads several times, and prodded with the stick some more, ignoring Nene's protests. "There," she said with one last twist, "I hope that teaches you a lesson."

We took him to a doctor later, and he took a dozen stitches, but no lesson was learned. He cut himself again and again, whenever he had a fight with Felicing, until crisscrossing scars, protruding like angry veins, adorned his middle. These elicited *ohs* and *ahs* of awe when he had his shirt off, providing fodder for conversation.

A tough woman was needed to match him. Once, after a quarrel, he went out to look for Felicing and found her on the beach. He took out his gun and fired at the glass of drink in front of her, splintering the glass and the group of people on the beach, but not her nerves. A worthy equal to his toys!

-    -   -   -

"You're coming tomorrow for dinner, right?" Nene asked as he put away his rifle.

"Yes, of course." My sisters had told me we were invited to the dinner at the villa that *Tio* Lorenzo and his wife *Tia* Piling were hosting the next night.

"Come early."

"Sure," I replied. "Let's drive over to Paquito's."

-    -   -   -

We found Paquito sprawled on a chair under the shade of a star-apple tree in front of their house. I watched him hurry over to the jeep when he saw us: tall, well built, green eyes, and like the rest of Jacinto Aberásturi's children, extremely good-looking. He was a couple of years older than myself and was the closest to me of all my cousins. Jacinto's father, Bruno Aberásturi, my father's oldest brother, married Justina Escaño, my mother's first cousin, which made Paquito and me related on both sides of the family.

Paquito's mother, Maria Javier, was as prolific as her sister, *Tia* Margarita, was barren. She gave Jacinto ten children, and it would be hard to find another house that produced as many beautiful people.

Once we were waiting outside the church for Mass to begin and I watched Tina, one of Jacinto's daughters, walking down the road under the acacia trees, looking like an angel in a white dress. Whenever she, or her sisters, ventured out of the house, a servant always walked behind, carrying a shielding umbrella. Tina greeted my father, kissed Mother and my sisters, and poked my tummy playfully with a finger. "Txomin," she said, her eyes sparkling as she teased me. She was something to behold, with her green eyes and white skin, her fair hair crowning her head like a halo, and a smile that stopped short the thudding of a young heart, the best-looking member of a family with an exorbitance of good looks. If my nine-year-old heart knew what a crush meant, it surely must have had one on Tina Aberásturi, although alas, *that* did not last long: she was a much older woman, already a teenager, and all that fluttering flickered to ashes when I myself became one.

- - - -

"So, when did you arrive?" Paquito asked, a greeting that needed no answer. Through the early morning grapevine, everybody knew who arrived in town and who left. He hopped into the jeep besides Nene, his body half in, half out of the vehicle, and we proceeded to the drugstore.

This was a favorite gathering place of cousins and friends, this drugstore, which we called the *esquina*. It stood on a corner lot; one side facing the house of Jacinto Aberásturi, the other side fronting the sea. It was owned by *Tio* Lorenzo's son, Matoy, and his pharmacist wife, and occupied the lower level of their house. Here, we would hang out for beer; those who cared to played *mahjong*, or a game of *burro*, and upstairs, the younger cousins very often held jam sessions.

On vacations, cousins would drive by late mornings, have a couple of beers, and the time would slip away in laughter and conversation. Most times, we would go down to the beach in front of the house, take a couple of laps in the sea, then it was time for lunch and a nap. Back again in the late afternoon, have another couple of beers, then home for dinner at 8.

-    -   -   -

Matoy had a bad heart and doctors said he would not live to see twenty. So as not to strain his heart more, *Tio* Lorenzo and *Tia* Piling made him quit school. They did not let him work and provided everything he needed, even after he married and had children, by which time, of course, he was a long way past twenty.

His life revolved around church. He attended Mass every morning and all that kneeling made his knees all dented and brown. He would stay in church long after Mass ended, and his wife had to send out a houseboy to remind him that Mass had been over a long time ago and it was time to come home.

He spent most afternoons playing *mahjong*, even when he started losing his eyesight, even after he lost it completely. So much practice when he still could see had made him perfect at the game. The saying "He could do it with his eyes closed," applied to him literally. He could play *mahjong* without looking. He knew exactly what tiles he had standing before him, and what tiles he had in his hand, by simply feeling them with his fingers. The other three players would announce what tiles they threw, but since Matoy had lost some of his hearing as well when he lost his eyesight, the games often became shouting matches, exercises in exasperation. There was not much to do when your eyes were useless and your heart was bad, however, so thank heavens for *mahjong*. His wife said the saint-makers up there would make him the patron saint of *mahjong* players when he went.

-    -   -   -

Mahjong was not the only game of diversion of the town. Others played tennis, gardened, or read. But to those who played *mahjong*, the game took on the proportions of a sickness that infected even those who had promised to live life in the service of God.

There was Father Genaro, for one, who made the game the ruling passion of his life, next to service to God, of course. After he finished his priestly chores, he went straight to the gambling houses in the neighboring towns and played high stakes *mahjong* until the wee hours. Once, some of my young cousins, who were learning to play the game, found themselves without a fourth player. They sought out Father Genaro and found him under the acacia trees outside the church.

"Come play *mahjong* with us, Father," they invited.

"For how much," Father Genaro asked.

"Five, ten centavos, Father," the girls replied.

"*Ay*," Father Genaro scoffed, shrugging his shoulders, his nose wrinkling in disdain. "*Maayo pa manginhas!*" (I'd be better off digging for clams!)

But the *mahjong* germs did not only live in small towns, they inhabited the big cities as well. In Cebu, Father Daniel, who came from faraway Ireland, often played with *Tio* Lorenzo's daughter, Milagros, games that lasted well unto the night. "Father," she once reminded him when a game was going well into midnight, "convent gates are closing soon."

"At this stage," he replied, "I'm past caring."

The gate to the Redemptorist convent closed at midnight and after a long *mahjong*-night out, Father Daniel had been known to scale the garden walls at dawn to gain entrance to the convent.

-    -   -   -

"What are you having?" I asked Paquito as I pulled up chairs. "Beer?" Of course he wanted beer, we all did. The girl minding the drugstore brought us a round of San Miguel beer and a couple of bowls of peanuts.

Mely Sala sauntered in and straddled a chair near mine. "Staying long?" he asked. He was a very close friend; we went way back when we were children.

"Just the week," I replied. "Beer?" I did not wait for his reply. I signaled the girl for another beer.

Mely Sala was as taciturn as Nene was articulate, taking in things around him without a word, the silent type who appealed to the ladies. He was an architect who did not curtsey to his clients. "So how much do you think this project will cost?" a client would ask, and get this terse reply, "Fifty thousand if you don't meddle, a hundred if you do." But he was the best in town, so his client would take this answer with a spoonful of sugar and say, "Well, that's Mely." If we did not pry him from his house, he sat in front of his drawing table, sketching lonely houses, drawing barren beaches, painting wasted landscapes.

If we poured a lot of liquid into him, however, we could get him out of his shell. Once out, he could be persuaded to sing. His song was always the same, "I Left My Heart in San Francisco." It was such hard work prying anything out of Mely that when he opened up, he always had an appreciative audience. That song was Mely's song. Even now, many, many years later, when I hear somebody sing that he left his heart in San Francisco, Mely Sala is up there with Tony Bennett in the pictures that spring to my mind. It was not San Francisco, though, but some golden, sunshiny town above the blue and windy sea, very much nearer home, where he later left his heart.

We were drinking our beers when Bingo, *Tio* Lorenzo's youngest son, came in, led by a houseboy.

"Hi, Bing," we greeted him.

He groped his way to each voice that greeted him, voices remembered from way back when his eyes did not trouble him as much, when he did not have to rely on voices or hazy features to recognize a face, did not have to wait for hands reaching out at him to answer a greeting.

"Hi, when did you arrive?" he asked me.

"This morning." I pulled out a chair for him.

"Staying long?" he asked.

"Just a week." I held the chair back and waited for him to be seated before I went back to my chair.

"What are you having?" Paquito asked.

"Coke," Bingo replied.

Paquito got up and got a bottle of Coca-Cola from the fridge. "Here's your drink, Bing, and peanuts." He put the bottle near Bingo's hand and moved the bowl of peanuts near him.

Sunlight glinted on my watch and drew my attention. "Oh, *Jeez*, I didn't realize how late it was. Mama's waiting lunch for me." This always happened when I was home. Time whizzed by and I was always late. I might as well not wear a watch here. I removed it and put it in front of Paquito. "I'll just take a quick dip," I told him.

The sea was a few feet away. I crossed the street, went down the short incline and the high tide met me. There was a narrow path here, a swath flanked with lush vegetation, where we used to slide down to get to the water when the tide was low. But there was almost no beach left when the water crested at high tide.

I took a few steps and the water rose up to my waist. I started to swim under; the water felt cold and good. I swam to the deeper part, feeling my muscles loosen with each stroke I took. How I missed this; I did not have a longing for the sea in other parts of my world. I had never been eager to accept invitations to outings to beaches. The few times I had, I just stayed on land with a bottle in my hand; somehow, no other sea held anything of interest to me.

There was no such thing as a quick dip when I was home. A few laps turned into several. As when I was a boy, I did not even want to come out. I could stay; no servant was going to call me. But Mother was waiting. So was lunch. I was ready for a good one after that long swim.

I came back up to the drugstore, picked up my towel and dried myself lightly. I liked the feel of whatever sea salt was left on my body after these swims. Tonight's bath would take care of whatever salt was left on my hair.

"I wonder how much this thing costs," said Paquito, swinging the strap of my Omega watch, one of the very few items of luxury I had allowed myself to indulge in.

"I have to go now. Mama is waiting." I said as I strapped on my watch. I turned to Nene. "Why don't you have lunch with us? Mama would be pleased."

"I have to go home," he replied.

"Want me to take you home now?"

"I'll take him home," volunteered Paquito, rising from his chair. I nodded and murmured thanks. He was such a pleasant person, very even-tempered, offering his services without being asked, was always there to help.

I placed a hand on Bingo's shoulder. "See you later, Bing." I turned to Mely. "Are you coming back this afternoon?"

"All right, if you are," he said.

-    -   -   -

I could not remember when I first became aware that *Tio* Lorenzo's younger sons were losing their eyesight. It was a slow, gradual process. Little by little, the eyeglasses became thicker and heavier, moving around became more difficult, reading became a thing of the past. Before we realized it, they had discarded the eyeglasses altogether. No more need. Then somebody had to read to them, the indispensable houseboy had to be there for them to hold on to when they navigated the streets. They were losing their eyesight, while I was sailing through life with them, and I was not particularly aware! It was like watching a baby grow into a boy, then into a lad. And then one day you look in amazement and wonder, *Where was I when all this was happening?*

First it was Roque, then Matoy, both older brothers. Now Bingo was going the same way. Not so long ago he could still negotiate the streets alone. This was a small town, people got out of his way, gave him room. Now, he depended on the ubiquitous houseboy. His family read about an eye doctor in Manila who had done wonders with people who had serious problems with their eyes.

But good as the doctor was, there was nothing he could do for Bingo. His tragedy was stamped in his genes; there was no human help for him.

It was selective, this insidious gene, sparing *Tio* Lorenzo's two daughters, Nenita and Milagros, sparing Ramon and Juan, the two oldest sons. But Roque and Matoy, and then Bingo, the younger sons, did not break away unscathed. Although through the years Juan's glasses became very thick, with designs on them like minute snowflakes, made especially for him by his eye doctor, at least he was spared from total darkness.

- - - -

When I arrived home, Mama and my sisters were already at table, waiting for me. Lunch was usual. Vegetable soup, *chuletas*-- -thick steaks of pork---and that old standby that I did not mind having any time, *tortilla de patata,* potato omelet. I had a treat after lunch, *borracho* that my sisters had made the day before. I loved this dessert---an icebox cake made with ladyfingers drenched with rum and topped with a milk-chocolate mixture.

After lunch we retired to our rooms for a brief rest. I had lost the habit of napping after lunch when I started working in the city. I brought in several magazines from the living room. Since the 1920s, Father had had a subscription to National Geographic, in addition to his subscriptions to other Spanish news magazines. He had a great interest in world events and had a short-wave radio that brought him news from all over the world. He read avidly the magazines Juanita subscribed to for him: *Time Magazine, Look, The Saturday Evening Post* and other magazines that were open to international subscriptions. He was therefore well informed and up-to-date on happenings around the world. His taste in books was wide-ranging; once, I saw him reading Jules Verne's futuristic literature with much enjoyment.

From him we got our love of reading, our love of books. We could not seem to go to bed, could not seem to prepare for sleep, could not seem to finish the day, without reading first. I picked up a National Geographic and settled myself in bed.

- - - -

I woke up with a jolt. The magazine I was holding had fallen to the floor. I rubbed the sleep off my eyes. I might have lost the habit of naps after lunch when I was away, but it caught up fast with me as soon as I came home.

10

Bees droned in the garden outside my window where Mother had planted a row of hydrangeas; million flowers, we called them, rich blue flowers clustered copiously on stems that bent with their weight. I dressed to go out. We very seldom used the front door when we went out. I passed through the dining rooms, and took the kitchen stairs. Mother was at a downstairs bedroom, her usual place at this time of day, listening to her radio, rolling her cigarettes. I sat down with her for a bit while we smoked her *buri* fabrication.

"Any girlfriends?" Mother asked.

I had a girlfriend here once. Mother did not like her. Then when we broke up, Mother liked her a lot. Girlfriends were not a good subject to talk about with Mother. I saw this new girl in the office. I could not help staring at her---beautiful legs, a cleft on her chin. I must have stared long because she shifted her gaze and looked at me. Then she smiled, and my ramparts came tumbling down, swept away like a castle of sand in the wind by a rush of emotion I had not felt in a long time. I wanted to sort out this curious sensation, but reined myself in. There was no sense in romanticizing *that*. I was preparing for this trip home, so that was that. *That* definitely was not a good subject to talk about with Mother. I hedged. "These cigarettes are good." A safe subject. "You know I always liked these even when I was little."

"Yes, aren't they?" She took one from the box where she kept them, lighted it and gave it to me. She looked me over. "You are not eating well. You are very thin."

"So are you. I guess I took after you."

"You are your father. At least there's something you got from me." The cigarettes were very slim, and did not take long to shrivel at the end. She lit another one and gave it to me. Mine was almost smoked out. "Going out?"

"I'm meeting Mely," I said.

"How's Mely?" She always liked Mely.

"Still the same." I finished my cigarette, rose and stretched. "I have to go. Bye, Ma." I kissed her forehead and remembered. "Oh, and thank you for the money for fare."

"If I don't send, you don't come."

"That's not true, not really," I laughed, "but, thanks."

-      -   -   -

Mely was already in the drugstore when I arrived.

Somebody mentioned that a movie was showing in the capital city where, in the middle, they had inserted pornographic segments. This we had to see for ourselves. We crowded into the jeep and sped to the capital.

We bought *siopao* from the Chinese restaurant before we entered the movie house, Chinese dumplings that stuck to a man's ribs more manfully than the skimpy popcorn, dumplings still hot from their baking places, with squares of baking paper stuck to their bottoms.

It was an awful movie. Even with the segments of half-naked men chasing naked women across the screen, segments from out of nowhere haphazardly inserted in the middle of a scene, it was still an appallingly bad movie. But we were young, and mesmerized, and did not watch what we were eating, until Mely started a commotion, clearing his throat noisily, *agh*, *agh*, trying to spit out we knew not what.

"What is it, what is it?" we chorused.

"*Peste*," Mely cursed between *agh*s, trying to expel the piece of baking paper from the bottom of the dumpling that now clung obstinately to his throat. We broke into peals of laughter that had the people around shushing us for quiet.

Pornography is best savored in silence, swirling its own fancies in the dark, low landscapes of the mind, and our bursts of hilarity broke the mood. That redeemed what otherwise would have been a dismal waste of an afternoon.

11

Sunday was always church day. We did not miss Mass unless we were terribly sick. Father was extremely religious and his deep faith was another quality that he handed down to his children. Since I was not planning on receiving Holy Communion---I did not go to Confession---I rose late and prepared to go to the second Mass. I ate breakfast alone; my mother and sisters were already in church. They always attended the first Mass. They took Holy Communion every time they heard Mass and this they could not do if they had already broken their fast. Church rule in those days.

"I shall be at the beach after church. Tell Mama I shan't be home for lunch," I told the maid.

- - - -

After church, I proceeded to the villa. Emit's house was on the way. After the war, with Lolita gone, he married again, had more children, and built another house not far from the villa. I decided to stop by after Mass.

Most Sunday mornings he would be in his garden, down among his plants, planting, replanting, weeding.

I couldn't drive fast; people walking home from church were taking their own sweet time, spread out on the road, talking, laughing, in no hurry to get home. I had to skirt the road slowly. No sense in dusting them in their Sunday best. Finally, I arrived at Emit's house and there he was in his garden, hunched, squatting over his plants in his dressing robe. Without his underwear. I parked the jeep by the side of the road and entered the gate.

"Morning, Mayor," I said. He had been the town mayor for a long time. Nobody had the money, or the clout, to oppose him.

"Hi, good morning," he stood up, smiling widely, obviously pleased to see me. He took my hand and put his arms around my shoulders. "When did you arrive? Come up, come up, let's have coffee."

"Thanks, I've had coffee, and a heavy breakfast, too," I said. I took out my cigarette, shook out a stick, and offered the pack to him, but he shook his head. I lighted mine, inhaled deeply, and said, "I'm going over to the villa. And you forgot your underwear again."

"I did?" He looked at me in all innocence, but couldn't hold it long. I had to laugh with him. He went about his house, and very often ventured outside, in his dressing robe, without his underwear, and sometimes even roamed the house without either.

Sunday mornings, when he was in his garden, he would make it a point to greet the ladies as they passed by after Mass. He especially liked to tease Ma'am Ilang, who had retired from teaching countless town children.

"Good morning, Ma'am Ilang," he would call out. Ma'am Ilang would glower at him, and return his greeting with an angry look.

He wondered, he would say with roguish glee, why the old ladies would glare at him when he greeted them and the younger ones would look hard, then would turn their heads away and titter. Then he would look down, he said, and oh my goodness, he chortled, he forgot to put on his underwear again. Shocking stern, everyday-in-church Ma'am Ilang was a Sunday treat for him.

"How's work in the big city?" he asked, patting my back.

"Ah," I said dismissively, "the question should be why work in the big city?"

"Because," he looked at me seriously, "you're a bright boy and a bright engineer and you'd be wasting your gifts in this small town."

I shrugged. "Oh, well, what you gonna do."

"You're going to the dinner tonight?" he asked.

"Yes, I am, of course."

"*Tia* Merced is going? I have not seen her in quite a while."

"You, and many others. No, I seriously doubt it" I said. "How are the children?"

"How else! Look at that one," he said. He nodded at the direction of a tree, where a boy was perched precariously on one of the branches.

"Hey," he called the boy, "Get down from there or you'll fall."

The misbehaving child went on with his business, ignoring his father completely.

"I said get down from there. Do you want a spanking?" he threatened, rearranging his face to match his voice, which face and voice the little scamp ignored. "All right, I'll count to three. If you're still there at the count of three, you'll get it. One, two, two and a half."

The boy just sat there on his branch, unmindful of the reprimand, clearly unafraid of the danger his father painted for him. Emit looked at me and laughed. "See what I mean?"

I remembered once he directed a dirty-faced son, "Go upstairs and tell the maid to wash your face." "I won't obey," challenged the errant boy. And again, there the matter rested. "*Con la cara feroz, basta,*" he summed up the scope of discipline he imposed in his house. With a ferocious face, that was enough, as far as discipline went. No, discipline was never his strong point. I had to laugh with him. I took a last draw on my cigarette and ground the butt with my shoes. "I have to go."

"I'll see you tonight then." He put his arm around my shoulders again, and walked me to the jeep.

I thought of Emit while I drove to the villa and I could not help but laugh. What a character he was. He had a *laissez faire* attitude about life that was quite remarkable. When a daughter from one of his many dalliances was in her early twenties, she had gone through a marriage and some other relationships that produced children by different men. But this state of affairs, considered scandalous at that time, did not trouble Emit. "Well," he would say with a shrug, "sex is good. We all enjoy it, don't we? Who doesn't?"

Who indeed! Not that he could have done anything about his children's values, even if he wanted to. The concept of being faithful to a spouse was foreign to him. He had liaisons with other women, some a-few-nights stands, others that lasted longer.

He lived an unstructured life while at the villa, unhampered by rules, pampered without boundaries by *Tia* Margarita, loved without conditions by *Tio* Agustin. With his good looks and his parents' money and power and position in the town propping him up, he roamed free and unrestricted. He did not know discipline and enforced none on his children.

- - - -

Nene was having breakfast when I came up the villa. "Come have breakfast," he invited.

"I've had, thanks," I answered.

"Coffee, then." He did not wait for my answer and turned to the maid. "Coffee for *Señorito* Txomin."

Done with breakfast, he turned to me, "Want to go to the beach?"

"I have my shorts and towel."

"All right then."

We passed by the marketplace and bought food and the requisite drinks. Then we picked up Paquito and Mely and drove to the beach at the outskirts of town. We spent many languid days on this beach, with our drink and our stories that bound us together through careless summers shared in lazy abandon.

I drove the jeep way under the trees. Straight ahead, the sea met the sky in a dazzling sheen, shimmering in the morning sun. The tide was not yet high enough; there was still a wide stretch of sand, then the crystal water ruffled softly as it lapped the sand at the edge of the tide-line. Even when the tide was at its highest, there would still be a spread of sand to lie on---one part open, golden and warmed by the sun, and another part, cool and in shadows, half-sheltered by the dense overhanging branches of the *talisay* tree.

A small boat skirted the water's edge. "Want some fish, *Señorito* Otic?" The fisherman rowing the boat asked. My cousins Otic Escaño and Juan Escaño had come and joined us.

"What have you got there?" Otic went over, looked over the fisherman's catch, and bought a bucketful, fish newly caught, some still wriggling inside the pail. The fisherman cleaned them out while Otic proceeded to build a fire and broil the fish.

I went into the water and took a long swim. The water, like the sand, was warm; I ventured into the deeper parts, letting my muscles loosen with each stroke I took. On my back, I let the water lull me gently, suspended on a dreaming daze, empty of thought, weightless of cares.

We lingered with the sun; loitered, ate and drank, and I caught up with Otic's *honest-to-God-true-story* stories. Usually, we would stay until the shadows chilled the beach and the first stars came out, wait for the moon to rise slowly from the sea, that fiery orange Malitbog moon, bigger than the one in Spain or in London, Father always said, wait until the orange lightened to pale yellow and flooded the beach with a ghostly whiteness. Then the church bells pealed the hour, and it was time for home and dinner.

Tonight, though, we were having dinner at the villa and we did not wait for the sun to withdraw. We wrapped up our afternoon, stashed our things into the jeep, and proceeded for home.

12

We were getting ready to go to the villa; at least I was ready. Juanita and Emiliana were still dressing up. Mother was at the small dining room, giving directions to the maids.

"Why don't you come tonight?" I coaxed her, knowing this was an exercise in futility. Never a social creature to start with, the long years of seemingly never-ending parties at the *Casa* took their toll. After my father took her away, she steered clear of social activities, did not even attend those parties that her first cousins threw, no matter that she liked *Tio* Agustin a lot, or that Father always went. Father gave up trying to get her to go, attended family parties with my sisters, went alone when he was invited by friends with whom he did business, and abandoned efforts to pry Mother out of the house and her self-imposed seclusion. With the exception of church, she had not been out in a long while.

"You know me. But you go and enjoy yourselves."

Yes, I knew her as well as I knew by heart the stories she told me at story-telling time, after lunch while the others were taking their naps. I would sit with her while she rolled her cigarettes, and listen to stories of her youth spent in the *Casa* after her parents died and the sister of her father, her aunt Agustina Faelnar Escaño, brought her and her siblings to live in the *Casa*.

She was treated like a daughter, her story went, fed, clothed, sent to school, provided for, but was expected to do more than the daughters---manage the household, supervise the servants, run the house. Her sister, Nena, also lived in the Casa, but Nena loved going out and partying, was as fun-loving as Mother was serious, and their aunt came to depend more and more on Mother.

She and her sister went to a boarding school in Manila. On holidays, she was her aunt's Girl Friday. Her duties were manifold, which she carried out assiduously. She checked that the servants did not loiter to gossip; she saw to it that money they borrowed was deducted from their weekly wages; she supervised the counting of the china and the glassware and the silverware before they were put away. A horde of servants lived in the servants' quarters somewhere in the recesses of the great house, but when a party was planned, and there often were parties, guests came in droves, and another horde of servants was hired for day service. This arrangement added a daunting task to Mother's duties: she must make sure these live-out servants did not take anything with them when they went home each night. They lined up in front of her before they left the house, and the searches were made, cursory no doubt, but nonetheless mortifying the searcher more than the searched.

No, Mother did not like going to parties. She'd had more than her share of parties while she was still living in the *Casa*. But though solitary, she did not settle in seclusion. She read, listened to her radio, listened to her thoughts. She loved going to plays presented in the capital city to which my sisters would take her, and took great delight in the plays that the family---my sisters and my cousins---put on in town. She enjoyed reading her Spanish magazines, which kept her informed on worldwide events that mattered to her. She loved listening to my sisters' accounts when they came home from affairs they had attended. Her radio kept her informed on what was happening on the national scene. Family members and my sisters' friends would come to visit; from them she learned the local news. *Tio* Agustin always passed by the house on his afternoon walks, and these visits she thoroughly enjoyed. With the daily dispatches that the housemaids dished out at mealtimes, she was quite up-to-date with the latest goings-on in town. These were all the matters she cared to know, more than these she did not care about. Her self-imposed isolation stemmed from other places buried inside her by a reserve nobody breached. No, parties she definitely could do without.

-     -   -   -

At last my sisters were ready. We took the jeep and proceeded to the villa.

Parties at the villa were the social events of the town and a flurry of preparation always attended them. Days before the party, servants from the villa would advise the town's butchers what dishes were going to be prepared, and by the time the big day arrived, the butchers had set aside what *Tia* Piling's cook needed. A sense of excitement always filled the night of the party.

- - - -

The entire length of the driveway was bright with lights. At the end of the driveway, the villa stood ablaze. I dropped my sisters in front of the house and steered the jeep to the side. I parked on a moonlit space, stepped out of the jeep, and lighted a cigarette. It was such a beautiful night I took my time, watching the moon cast shadows on the flowers, breathing in deeply the scents of summer. A muted sigh passed through the trees as a slight breeze rustled softly through the leaves, shivering with moon-silver glints under the shimmering sky. I enjoyed my cigarette slowly until the end shriveled to mere ash; then I went up the house.

Tio Lorenzo and *Tia* Piling and their family had been staying in the villa since before the war. Much later after the war, they built a huge house next to the villa, but had not occupied it yet, reluctant to leave *Tio* Agustin alone, now that Lolita, and of course *Tia* Margarita, were not there anymore.

Tio Agustin, standing at the top of the stairs, looking dapper in a white linen suit, greeted me as I came up.

"So, Txomin, you're home," he said as he patted me on the back.

"Good evening, *Tio*. Yes, I'm home for the week," I replied.

"Good evening, *Tio*," Juanita and Emiliana came over to greet him. They started talking while I stood quietly on the side watching *Tio* Agustin. It had been a long time since *Tia* Margarita died but he never got over that tragedy and never married again. I thought of *Tia* Margarita and the events of her death that left a very strong impression on me, so strange, to still remember when I was then only four years old.

Mother had household needs that she could not find in the stores in town. Every once in a while, she would go to Maasin, the capital city, to shop for the bulk of our needs. Occasionally, she would go with *Tia* Margarita and *Tio* Agustin in their car, a Studebaker *El Presidente*, very big and capacious, but this Mother did not do often. She liked to take Ramon and me with her on these outings and I was impossible in the confines of a car.

On this eventful day, Mother had bought all she needed. *Tio* Agustin, also in the city at the time, came over to where we were waiting for the bus.

"Do you have a ride?" he asked Mother.

"We're taking the bus today," Mother replied.

"No, you're not," said *Tio* Agustin, "the car is here. Come with us."

"No, Agustin, not today," Mother said firmly.

Seeing how Mother was more burdened than usual with packages and my brother and me in tow, *Tio* Agustin insisted. There were only three of them, he said, *Tia* Margarita, her sister-in-law *Señora* Cleta Javier, and himself.

"Come, Ced, the ladies will be very happy to have your company. There's so much room in the car, and you know I never mind the children." Meaning us. "Right, Txomin?" He rumpled my hair playfully, dipped his hand in the pocket of his pants and came up with some lemon drops, which he gave to Ramon and me. We thanked him happily. He always had *caramelitos,* small candies, in his pocket that he would give us children when we came visiting.

"Come on, Ced," he coaxed again.

But Mother did not want to impose on other people an unruly four-year-old who could not keep still. Meaning me. On this she was adamant.

"Next time, Agustin, I promise. And thanks." Married to a Basque for a long time, she had become like one herself; when her mind was made up, little could dissuade her.

In the end, *Tio* Agustin relented, and on the bus we went.

On the way home, we passed a commotion on the road. People were milling about, whispering to each other excitedly. The bus stopped and we heard fragments of conversation: the Escaño car, an accident.

We must have gotten down from the bus; Mother must surely have wanted to talk to *Tio* Agustin. I could not now recall. What came to mind when I thought of this incident was *Señora* Cleta looking out the window of the car, her face bloody from a gash across her cheek.

We later learned that their car, swerving to avoid an oncoming vehicle, had gone off the road, and fallen into a culvert. *Tia* Margarita died later of diabetic complications from wounds sustained in the accident.

I had wondered what would have happened to me had Mother accepted *Tio* Agustin's invitation and we had gone with them in their car. Thin little boy that I was, squirming out of arms that would restrain me, surely I would have gotten more than just a gash in the face. And I thought, unruly was not bad, after all.

Such a long time ago, but as I watched *Tio* Agustin, I thought, no, not that long ago; pain stayed fresh and raw when there was nothing to replace that loss.

-   -   -   -

Tia Piling and *Tio* Lorenzo came over and greeted us: *Tio* Lorenzo quite debonair in white, *Tia* Piling elegant in formal clothes. In these parties, the ladies were always in their stylish best, in dresses that were almost always new, planned and executed weeks before the event.

"So Txomin, you're home," *Tio* Lorenzo said. "A game of *burro*?"

"Anytime you want, *Tio*, just send for me."

When Father was still alive, he and *Tio* Lorenzo would play a game called *burro* with a couple of other friends. Now that Father was not here anymore, I took his place when I was home.

Drink in hand, I moved about, listening to the talk and laughter as everyone greeted one another. I could see Nene in one corner, talking to my sisters, and Emit, in the center of a group, regaling his audience with stories about politics. I shied away from that. I picked at some *hors d'oeuvres* to go with my drink, while I answered the same question: *When did you arrive? How long are you staying?* Then, *Good to see you home.*

At last dinner was announced.

This was how it always was at parties in this house. The long table was laden with dishes of pork and beef and chicken and fish and various Spanish dishes. On another table was an array of *postres*, sweets to close down the appetite. I seldom touched the other scrumptious desserts on the dessert table. I had a simple sweet tooth that could be soothed with chocolates, and tonight with *flan*, custard that felt like silk on the tongue. Very often at these parties, my appetite had been closed long before I reached the other end of the dessert table.

The party went on long unto the night, friends and cousins had an enormously great time, and reluctantly, we let the evening slip away.

Yes, it was good to be home.

13

I spent the next morning puttering about the house and the grounds. The flowers were in full bloom, crowding out leaves and stems on branches. Trees were heavy with fruit. Buzzing bees hovered on blue blossoms, humming commentaries in silver notes. Butterflies feasted on gardenias, their wings gossamer on the white petals. Somebody writing about chaos suggested that a butterfly fluttering its wings in China could trigger a hurricane in the Atlantic. I wondered in which part of the world all these fluttering wings would cause a turmoil in the weather, or which part of the world fluttering butterflies caused the upheavals in my part of the world. Not likely though, I thought. Not very likely.

I paused under the mango tree. I recalled the day such as this when Ramon decided to prune a branch of the tree that was arching away from the trunk. With a saw tied to his waist, he climbed up the tree and facing the tree trunk, sat on the branch he wanted to cut back. He proceeded to saw the limb from the tree. The bough creaked, split, broke away from the trunk, and plunged, carrying my brother, astride the severed branch, down to the ground. Amidst a huge commotion of branches and leaves, my brother's body hit the hard earth. A familiar Ramon moment, dangerously abstracted, incredibly inattentive.

Yellow fruit spotted a guava tree. I lowered my head, brushed aside a branch and reached up to pick a low-hanging fruit, golden and large and firm, just perfect for eating today; tomorrow would find it too ripe. I broke a branch with a couple of leaves and a fruit at the end and went to the house to look for Mother. She was at the downstairs bedroom, as usual, quietly smoking. I handed her my offering.

"You smoke too much," I said.

"So do you," she said.

I picked up one cigarette from her box and lit it. We stayed that way, puffing silently.

I loved these quiet moments with her. When I was younger, we would smoke while she would tell me stories of her own youth, of her cousins. I remembered I asked her once why Otic Escaño lived with *Tia* Piling and *Tio* Lorenzo and not with his own parents.

"Because his parents are separated," she answered. They had been separated a long time, but there is no divorce in the Philippines. People fall out of love; some remain married despite. He would just find himself another woman on the side, she would just find herself another man. Or stay, and find something to nag and be bitter about.

Mother then told me the sad story of *Tio* Nemesio Escaño, Otic's father. *Tio* Nemesio, like his older brothers *Tio* Lorenzo and *Tio* Agustin, and his other siblings, studied in Spain, too. While there, he met *Tia* Antonina, married her, and brought her with him when he came back to Malitbog.

Their marriage was rocky from the start. He was a gentle, quiet gentleman; she was a rambling, never-still woman.

Managing the household fazed her. The fact that she never bothered to learn even just the rudiments of the local dialect did not make things any easier for her. She muddled through simple housekeeping tasks with much lamentation, and made small hills of mundane housework into insurmountable mountains that she expected *Tio* Nemesio to scale. Catering to the wishes of an adored wife gave *Tio* Agustin much pleasure. For *Tio* Nemesio, however, wishes seemed like capricious whims when love had lost its shine.

Tia Antonina would be at our house often to unburden herself to my father and *Tio* Nemesio would bring his complaints to my mother, confidences that often saddened her.

"I'm just tired, Ced," he told my mother once. "I'm tired of doing everything for everybody, of having to be there all the time for everyone," *Tio* Nemesio said wearily. "Of course there are servants, but the good ones never stay, the way she treats them. Those who do stay have to be managed or they don't get anything done. She just does not understand that that's why these people work as servants. If they knew better, they would not be here working for us. And her incessant complaints! Everything is just way over her head.

"Yesterday, she wanted to make a pillowcase. She came out carrying a piece of pattern paper, all the while complaining about the pattern and the paper. Needing a pattern to make a pillowcase? How hard is it to make a pillowcase? Even I could make a pillowcase. But I don't dare say that, or I'd end up making the thing myself. And the worst thing is, she never finished it. It was just too much for her, a pillowcase!"

Mother laughed at this, but it was more sad than funny. He was starving for a peaceful life, but peace and quiet was just beyond his reach. In the end, he found himself another woman, left his wife and moved to another town across the bay.

When he left, his mother, Agustina Faelnar Escaño, made it known that she was leaving *Tia* Antonina as much money as she was leaving her own daughters, hoping that this would entice her son to come back to his wife and children. But to come back, even to all that money, was just unacceptable to *Tio* Nemesio, and he stayed away.

When she resigned herself to the fact that her husband was never coming back to her, *Tia* Antonina went to Manila to live with her only daughter, leaving behind her three sons in the care of *Tio* Lorenzo and *Tia* Piling, and also of *Tio* Agustin, as all of them lived in the villa. The two older ones, Fernanding and Fermin, worked in one or other of the Escaño ships; Otic, much younger, became another son to *Tio* Lorenzo and *Tia* Piling. They sent him to school at the Jesuits' Ateneo de Manila with their own son, Juan, and a strong bond developed between the two cousins---a bond of shared blood, enduring friendship, and a remarkable propensity to drink.

Meanwhile, *Tio* Nemesio had children with the other woman, children who stayed on the outer fringes of the family life, recognized as Escaños, but not fully tasting the advantages that came with that name.

The family later learned that *Tio* Nemesio had contracted consumption. He would go to Cebu for cures, but these were futile efforts. When later Mother learned that he was going back to Cebu in one of the Escaño ships, most probably for the last time, she boarded the ship when it passed by Malitbog and had one last talk with this cousin who was very close to her. *Tio* Nemesio died shortly after that. At last he came back to Malitbog, to be buried in the family mausoleum.

-   -   -   -

"Going for a swim?" Mother now asked me, throwing a glance at the towel slung over my shoulder.

"I'll go to the villa first. Then I'll take a quick dip, just in front of the *esquina*."

"You need it. You're too white," she observed.

"I won't take long. I'll be back for lunch. Bye, Ma."

-   -   -   -

The morning was stifling. I unbuttoned my shirt as I ran up the steps of the villa. I could hear voices in the other part of the house, but the living room was empty. I went straight to Nene's bedroom.

We stayed there for the rest of the morning, looking at his guns again, not doing much else, just catching up on lost time, while he brought me up to date on the more personal affairs that concerned the family. We could spend the time talking about anything or everything, or let time slip by in comfortable silence, covering as much in silence as in conversation, while the topics and time seamlessly flowed. Then it was time for lunch.

"I have to go." I picked up the pack of cigarettes I had placed on his table.

"Have lunch first."

"Mama is expecting me. You know, short vacation."

I passed by the drugstore on the way home; there was nobody around. I parked the jeep on the side of the road and surveyed the sea before me, the waves rippling with the breeze, the water gleaming under the sun.

I always felt, whenever I leave this town, that I leave behind a part of myself, and what I leave I could not find anywhere, in all the other places I searched.

I marveled at these strings that pulled us to this place, that bound our feelings of content, even of this thing called happiness, firmly to these waters and this patch of earth, these threads that were woven so inexorably through the fabric of our lives and covered us with this longing to stay, steeped us with this regret to leave.

-    -   -   -

I stripped my shirt off, climbed out of my jeans, and flung my sandals to the back seat. Then I slipped down the incline to the beach.

The water was high and I swam to the farther end. I went under with my eyes wide open as I did as a boy, checked seaweeds floating in front of my face, stared down a fish staring at me, extended my hand quickly to grasp it but it wiggled quickly away, too elusive for me. I burst out of the water to catch my breath, then plunged back down again, did underwater cartwheels, reliving pleasures that enveloped me when I was a boy, in this silent, well-remembered, ethereal sea.

I came up with my shorts dripping heavily. I squeezed out the seawater a bit and headed for home. I was feeling very good, feeling great, in fact, with the sun reaching in and warming my bare body, a breeze wafting my hair dry.

So who's to say when childhood's over?

14

By late afternoon I left the house for the *esquina*. Juan Escaño, Otic Escaño and some other cousins were already at the pier in front of the drugstore. Usually, they preferred the marketplace, where they could have some *tapas* to go with their San Migs. There were times when they changed venues and carted themselves happily to Matoy's drugstore, and their bottles to the pier. When too many bottles were transported, they would leave their inhibitions and their clothes on the shore and plunge into the water naked. Or, bottles in hand, they would tell stories tall or short. Otic's tall stories were taller than the others', and when he ended them with "*cross my heart, hope to die, true story*," nobody disputed him. These stories became part of family lore.

The laughter on the pier carried well past the drugstore. I asked the girl minding the store for a bottle of San Miguel and brought my bottle over to the pier. Pieces of clothing were scattered on the sand.

I remembered the last time I was here.

Somebody had made a dare, and Juan, with his system full of drink, did not let it pass. He jumped from the pier into the water and stayed there until the other cousins fished him out, dripping wet. They brought him up to Matoy's house, helped him remove his wet clothes and put him to bed. In the state he was in, the other cousins decided it was better he just spent the night there.

The next day he was sober and dry, but his clothes were not. The housemaids had collected all pieces-for-laundry on the floor to wash. What to do? He was a tall man, and big, and his brother Matoy was not, and it was time to go home. Nobody was up and about in Matoy's house who could drive him home. But the sun was already up and glaring, and the day was getting old. He put on Matoy's raincoat, the only thing he could fit into in the closet.

He trudged home in the dazzling sun, covered up in rain gear that was too short for him, a good part of his naked legs sticking out from under the raincoat. Whom should he meet on the road but his mother? He was too embarrassed to greet her and hoped she was too dumbfounded to address him and that maybe mother and son could pass like strangers in the noonday sun. No such luck!

"Juaning," *Tia* Piling demanded, "what are you doing in that raincoat?"

"I feel sick, Mama," he mumbled under his breath, "and I am cold," or something to that effect, leaving his mother too astonished for words.

Ah, a cousin after my own heart.

15

When gold was found in Panaon Island across the bay, the craze for gold reached fever pitch in our town. *Tio* Lorenzo, Father, and some of their friends founded the Royal Gold Mine Exploration to mine the gold.

"This will bring in a lot of money," said Tingting Faelnar, a lawyer for *Hijos* and one of the investors in the new corporation that held such golden prospects. "A lot of money. Bi..bi..bi..billions," he sputtered, jumping over millions in his excitement.

Even Mother, that reclusive soul who had to be dragged to get her out of the house, went out with her friend, our neighbor Na Juling, and panned the riverbed for gold. They scrutinized rocks and stones and when they saw minute rivulets of glitter in them, would bring their find home to show to my amused father.

Tio Lorenzo sent his son Juan to America, to the Colorado School of Mines in Golden, Colorado, to study the intricacies of the mining operations. Juan had by this time already graduated from Ateneo de Manila with a degree in Accounting.

Off to Colorado Juan went. But it did not take long for him to tire of the mining business, its billions of promises notwithstanding. He spent more time in the bars than in the schoolrooms and, with shades of history, *Tio* Lorenzo ordered him to come home or have his allowance cut off. But Juan was not about to be ordered back to a small town when the bars of America beckoned. He and another Filipino named Teofisto, whom he met while at the Colorado School of Mines, drifted from bar to bar to Detroit. There, life held if not more meaning, surely more excitement. They hopped from one bar to another, where Teofisto, like most Filipinos who needed just the slightest prodding to sing, sang, and Juan, who was an excellent piano player, played the piano and sang, too. Juan had an astonishing repertoire of songs which he sang while accompanying himself on the piano, from operatic arias to songs from Broadway musicals---from Coward to Romberg and Friml, to songs by Gershwin, Berlin, Porter, Kern, to tunes by less elite composers but which nevertheless became classics entrenched in the American song catalog. Juan and Teofisto were a good team, the free drinks sent over by appreciative listeners were ample, the money dropped into the hat on top of the piano was generous. But as excitement in any field must ebb, so did that of the song-and-piano routine. Eventually, Juan packed up his nomadic life, came back to Cebu, and worked as an accountant for *Hijos* until the war came and went, and with it, whatever profitability *Hijos* in Cebu enjoyed.

Then he came back home to Malitbog,

He worked as the company accountant when *Tio* Lorenzo and Father founded L. Escaño and Company. Now he was the accountant accountable to his father.

Tio Lorenzo would give him reports to be finished in a definite time. But the marketplace with its drinking places, where his cousin, Otic Escaño, and a bottle or two, (well, really more than three, oh, all right, much, much more than four,) and the prospect of a spirited discussion waited, was a lure more compelling than any project his father pressed on him. Juan would pass by the marketplace with the good intentions of having just one for the road. But the road was long. So were the discussions, and he and Otic would have another for another road, and yet another, while the argument became more heated and wide-ranging, from politics to religion to whatever came to mind.

Otic just waited for Juan to open a topic, then he would pounce and dispute the first sentence. "That's not how it happened," or "That's a stupid way of looking at things," and off they went, galloping into a debate that went nowhere. On one such argument, to stress a point, Otic pounded his fist on the table, right on Juan's eyeglasses that rested on the wooden surface, cracking the lenses. Juan went around town peering at the world through eyeglasses crisscrossed with cracks until replacement arrived.

Juan would disappear for a day or two, to reappear before *Tio* Lorenzo, wine-filled and empty-handed. *Tio* Lorenzo would roar at him. "You're fired."

"You cannot fire me," Juan, plastered, would shoot back in indignation, "because I quit. I resign." A day or two later, clearheaded and quiet as he typically was when he was sober, Juan would be back at his desk, putting to rights the accounts of the company. Until the next time.

16

Who can explain what strange chemical makeup inside us draws us to one person and not the other? Then again, maybe it's not so much chemistry as being thrown together too often, to the exclusion of others, that makes cousins fall in love with cousins.

We had always been a very insular family, probably because there were so many of us, and we were sufficient unto ourselves. When school was out, cousins from other provinces flocked to Malitbog and cousins organized picnics and dinners and parties among themselves. Rumors were rife in our town of strange goings-on when these cousins were together in the evenings, lighting bonfires on the beach, swimming in the moonlight. Of course these rumors reached Father's ears. It could not have been lost on him that Juan Escaño had started to show signs that he was favoring Cristina over the other cousins, and though my parents were very disturbed to see him gazing at Cristina with looks that definitely were not cousinly, they were more disturbed to see that she seemed to return the sentiment.

Father was very strict with his daughters, more so once they had grown into young adults. He instituted curfews for them, which, like the other rules he imposed in our house, were never questioned. He outlawed moonlight swimming, and not one of them entertained the notion of going out on black nights when there was no moon at all. Of course they did not go out often, and never alone; one of them always chaperoned the other. My parents hoped that the less Juan Escaño presented himself before Cristina, the less he would linger in her mind. Maybe it worked. She confessed to Mother that there was a gentleman who was interested in her, a Roces from Manila. At least, my parents hoped, he would divert her attention from Juan Escaño.

-     -   -   -

Then a propitious thing happened. The mayor of Cebu City, and Sergio Osmeña Junior called on *Tio* Lorenzo. Sergio Osmeña Junior was a son of a former Philippine President. At a later time, he would become one of the country's senators, but for now, he and the mayor wanted my sister, Cristina, to be Miss Cebu at the Cebu Carnival, a celebrated annual affair that drew people from all over the country.

Our parents were very retiring people and Cristina was just as reticent. She had always been beautiful even as a child; now she had grown into a willowy, stunning woman. Her beauty could not have been lost on her, but she did not give it much mind. Over the years, Mother, in little but persistent ways, slowly impressed on her daughters that beauty was just a gift not to be overly proud of, certainly not as much to be nurtured as an upright character. These lessons dripped steadily into Cristina's subconscious, so that when Sergio Osmeña Junior asked *Tio* Lorenzo to intercede with Father, Cristina cried. "Please, Papa, I don't want to." But Sergio Osmeña Junior was a very good friend of *Tio* Lorenzo's and *Tio* Lorenzo did not quite know how to refuse him. *Tio* Lorenzo pleaded with Cristina and she did not quite know how to refuse *Tio* Lorenzo, either. In the end she acquiesced and Father gave reluctant permission. "As long as we don't have to pay for her gown. That must cost a fortune," said Father. Sergio Osmeña Junior was happy they got the girl; the gown was the least of their concerns. Cristina reigned, and there Cesar Lopez saw her. They met again in another party and he started courting Cristina in earnest.

He would call on her at Emiling Aberásturi Gonzalez' house in Cebu where Cristina stayed, and sometimes, when *Tio* Lorenzo and *Tia* Piling were there visiting, too, *Tio* Lorenzo would sit at the piano and invite Cesar to sing. He could not sing that well, but he was a very self-assured man. He had an easy charm about him, the manner of the financially privileged that showed in the sure and confident way he moved. No, he did not need much invitation to sing. Looking at Cristina, he would spread his arms wide and burst forth into a Franz Lehar song, to *Tio* Lorenzo's accompaniment, and the others' amusement. "*Yours is my heart alone.*" That was his favorite song. Embarrassed, Cristina would cover her face with her hands and run to her room.

It was a slow process for her, returning the affection Cesar Lopez obviously felt for her. Maybe she realized how unwise that course with Juan Escaño was, or maybe our parents just implemented enough preventive measures to cool down young people's blood. Whatever the case, Juan Escaño, now seldom seen, slowly receded into the background. Still, there was the Roces guy, handsome enough to turn any girl's head, still very much there, still actively pressing his suit. Then one day in church, head bowed, Cristina prayed for guidance, looked up, and there Cesar Lopez was, taking Holy Communion. For a girl who did not make major decisions without first praying to the Virgin Mary for guidance, this was as sure an answer as she could hope for and would forever change the landscape of her heart.

With Cristina out of his world, Juan Escaño turned his attentions on Juanita. But Juanita was made of different stuff. Juan Escaño's overtures did not make the slightest dent even on the outermost periphery of her heart.

- - - -

It was welcome news to Father, then, that gentlemen guests were coming from another island across the sea to visit Cristina, gentlemen guests not having Aberásturi or Escaño tucked into their names. Cesar Lopez and his cousin Charlie Ledesma were coming to visit and stay at our house for a few days.

Ramon and I were on top of a *tambis* tree eating the red fruits, our lips and faces puckered from the unripe, sour fruit, when Cesar Lopez and Charlie Ledesma arrived. "Hey, boys," said Cesar Lopez, looking up at us. "That looks good, what is that? Could you drop some for us?" We ignored him and kept on eating. Cesar stooped down, picked up a stone, and threw it at us, missing widely. This was our introduction to our would-be brother-in-law.

We always used the large dining room when we had guests. Things were at their usual best, the long table wore an embroidered cloth, the silver gleamed, the crystal shone. Everything was perfect. Except for Ramon and me.

Our guests came from one of the wealthiest families in the country, owned lands planted mostly in sugar cane, owned a shipping line, things like that. But Ramon and I owned the *tambis* tree outside, and this house, and the food being served.

We piled our plates with food so our guests could not have seconds. When fruit was served, we helped ourselves to as much as our plates could carry, leaving a pittance for our guests. Of course we bit off more than we could chew; the maids took away our plates still heaped with food. All this was not lost on Father.

One night, after dinner, a maid placed a platter of papaya slices on the table. Although we did not particularly care that much for papaya, Ramon reached over and piled his plate with papaya slices. I followed suit, leaving a few sorry slices on the platter, and with chin held high, looked at our guests impudently.

Father made a don't-touch-it gesture to the maid when she came to collect our plates. Then he looked at Ramon and me and said, "You two don't leave the table until you have finished all the food on your plates."

"I'm full, Papa," said Ramon.

"I'm full, too, Papa," I echoed.

"I said not until you two have finished all the food on your plates," Father said quietly. When Father took this ominous tone, even I shut up and obeyed. It was not much fun after that, if we had to gorge on food we did not care for too much. Thus ended our short career feuding with Cesar Lopez.

17

December 8, 1941! The Japanese bombed Pearl Harbor!

We were at breakfast when we heard the news over Father's radio. Ten hours after Pearl Harbor, the Japanese also bombed American naval facilities in the Philippines: the base in Angeles, Pampanga, and Nichols' Air Base. "I'm afraid America will be drawn into war this time," said Father grimly.

"What does that mean, Papa?" we asked.

"It means that if America enters the war, war will surely follow here." The Philippines was at this time a protectorate of the United States.

To add to our apprehension, my sisters Juanita, Emiliana and Clotilde were still at the boarding school in Cebu.

"How are we going to get the children out and bring them home?" asked Mother, worry knitting her brows.

Then we heard somebody shouting. "*Señor*, the Japanese are already here!" Through our window we could hear commotion outside. One of Father's workers was shouting, "*Señor*, they're here!"

"What?" Father hastily rose from the table and looked out the window.

"*Señor,* a boat is approaching the pier. And they say it's full of Japanese soldiers."

Father hurried out the door, dashed down the porch steps, with Ramon and me close behind him. I did not know whether to be afraid or thrilled. But I could not be fearful. Father was purposely striding towards the enemy invasion with me beside him, excited but unafraid.

I had no idea how Father felt about the Japanese. There was just one lone Japanese in our town, Kato, the baker, who supplied us with delicious bread. I did know, though, how much he abhorred Hitler and the Germans, Mussolini and Franco. Time and again, I had heard him get furious whenever those names were mentioned and spoken of with admiration by his friends, other Spaniards who lived in Leyte and Cebu and who were also involved in the abaca and copra business.

Even before war broke out in Europe, and Japan entered into an alliance with Germany and Italy, even when the clouds of war were just hovering darkly over that continent, my parents were already aware that something horrible loomed on the horizon. *Tio* Lorenzo, *Tio* Agustin, and Father had their ears glued to their short-wave radios, to the British Broadcasting Corporation (whose broadcasts we called the gospel according to the BBC), scanning European stations for news, fearfully watching Germany's moves. Some evenings, Father's friends---fellow Spaniards who made their living dealing in the abaca business---would visit Father and *Tio* Agustin and *Tio* Lorenzo, sometimes at our house, sometimes at the villa. When they did, a spirited discussion always followed. Father, who was Basque, and *Tio* Agustin and *Tio* Lorenzo, who went to school and spent a good part of their youth with family in Spanish Basque land, staunchly supported the Allies. It was, after all, Hitler's arms and Stuka dive bombers that bathed Guernica and the Basque lands in blood, and put Franco in power, a power that he later used to suppress the insular Basques and everything they stood for.

Some of these Spanish friends were not Basques, however, and therefore shared the same sentiments towards Franco as other non-Basque Spaniards did. They called themselves Franquistas, grateful to Franco for uprooting the Spanish Republican Government, standing on the other end, rooting for the Nationalist rebels during the Spanish Civil War. They supported Franco's dictatorship, and consequently sympathized with Germany. Later, when Hitler's forces rampaged into Europe and Germany's allies ravaged Spain and the Philippines, these Franquistas did a complete turn-around once they grasped what Germany and Japan were about, and they finally faced the horror that was war.

When these Spanish friends visited, we went with Father to the villa. I would sit at his feet, or play with my cousins, while my ears absorbed what they argued about. Though I could not fully understand the words, I could recognize the apprehension behind them.

Father could not forget how he had to fetch my sisters Cristina and Juanita from war-torn Spain. He could not forget the horrifying accounts of the bombing of the defenseless town of Guernica, a walking distance from his own village of Forua, how Guernica was pounded to rubble by three hours of incendiary bombing, how the hamlet burned for three days, and most unforgivably, how the German pilots of the Condor Legion strafed the women and children running out of the burning town, flying down so low that they could be seen laughing when the women and their children dove into the ditches along the roadside embankments, how pieces of bodies were scattered everywhere. These were his own people, his childhood friends, his neighbors and relations! No wonder his blood boiled whenever Hitler or Franco was mentioned.

-   -   -   -

It was eerily quiet as we approached the pier. People crouched under the wooden pier; men and women watched silently from shore as a lumbering boat approached. About twenty to thirty yards from the end of the pier, a pile of sand bags had been built, behind which about half a dozen Filipino soldiers holding rifles and a machine gun hunkered down in a trench. A young American officer stood behind them, binoculars to his eyes.

"What have we here?" Father addressed the young officer.

"Don't go any farther!" the officer admonished. "We fear a Japanese contingent is about to attempt a landing on the pier. I've already sent to the barracks for reinforcements."

"Are you sure those are Japanese?" Father countered.

"Last night we received a report that all inter-island shipping has been banned from sailing, and we were cautioned to be on the lookout for enemy attempts to land on any of the outlying coasts. We improvised this trench and we've been here since then."

Father appealed to the officer, "Please hold your fire. That ship looks familiar to me." He was looking intently at the approaching vessel, getting quite excited. "In fact," his voice rose a few notches, "in fact, I believe it's one of our ships plying between Cebu and the outlying towns of Leyte."

"But how can it be here when all ships were banned from leaving Cebu?" the officer wondered.

"That ship takes bout 12 hours to get here from Cebu," Father informed the officer. "Probably it left Cebu between five and six yesterday afternoon, long before the orders were given to stop all ships from leaving." Then he decisively stepped out in front of the sandbags, with Ramon and me beside him. The early morning sun shone bright on his silver hair. Suddenly, from the ship, which was quite near now, we saw hands and arms waving and I recognized my own sisters.

"Papa, Papa," I exclaimed, just as excited, "those are the girls, Papa."

Father looked intently at the ship and when he saw Emiliana, Juanita and Clotilde waving at us, he burst out laughing. Turning towards the officer, he said, "Lieutenant, those are my three daughters who are supposed to be at the boarding school in Cebu." Then his brows furrowed. "But how come they're here?"

By then, people had come up and started to fill the pier. My sisters were among the first to come down the gangplank. They rushed towards us laughing and chattering like magpies.

"I'm happy to see you, of course," Father greeted them. We were kissing and laughing, relieved that they made it home safely. "But what are you doing here?"

"*Tia* Toyang was about to board the ship to come home when she remembered us," they chorused. *Tia* Toyang was a sister of *Tio* Lorenzo. "Then she went to see Mother Superior. *Tia* Toyang told her that you had asked her to get us so we could all take the ship which had a special permit to sail for Malitbog. So, here we are!"

"Bless Toyang!" father breathed.

"There she is now!" my sisters cried happily.

Tia Toyang was coming down the gangplank. They rushed to help her down and Father embraced her. "Thanks for thinking of the girls."

As we passed by the sandbags, Father addressed the young American officer, "Thank you for holding your fire."

The young man blushed and, laughing, answered, "We weren't really going to fire unless they fired at us first."

-    -   -   -

The Second World War already raged in Europe and although the Japanese had not yet occupied our town, they had begun to throttle life in other parts of the land. They expropriated, or just stranded, the regular inter-island transportation that was the lifeblood of the islands composing the country, transportation without which no commerce and indeed, no livelihood, could survive.

In April of 1942, Cesar Lopez came back to Malitbog in a boat with his friend, Doctor Ismael Reynoso, to marry Cristina. They had a big wedding. We held the celebration on our front lawn. A couple of cows and several pigs were slaughtered for the wedding feast, and the townspeople shared in the festivities.

Father did not want to send his daughter away alone, to another island with a different dialect, to a slew of Lopezes we hardly knew, to a family whose lavish lifestyle was so unlike our own. Juanita and Emiliana went back on the boat with Cristina and Cesar, to the *hacienda* outside Bacolod City called Bayabas that the Lopezes owned. There Juanita and Emiliana stayed for over a year, so that only my parents, Clotilde, Ramon, and myself were left in our house when the first contingent of Japanese arrived in our town.

-    -   -   -

The Japanese came to town in four large trucks. They immediately occupied the *Casa* and made it their headquarters. Some members of *Tio* Lorenzo's family, and his sister, *Tia* Toyang, were living in the *Casa* at the time. The severity of the situation had not yet sunk into *Tia* Toyang's head when the soldiers came marching up the *Casa*.

"*Que simpaticos, que simpaticos,*" she gushed.

How she found charming a troop of invaders tramping into the house with neither invitation nor permission was beyond comprehension. Then one of them, with the arrogance of the armed lording it over the helpless that would later become a constant in our lives, looked at *Tia* Toyang, pointed to his lap, and commanded, "Sit." There their charm ended.

"*Que animales, que animales!*" *Tia* Toyang later raged.

I often wished I was there and witnessed what must have been drama of the highest order---the high and mighty *Tia* Toyang, giver of imperious orders, herself being ordered to sit on the lap of this foreigner who, in normal times, would not have merited a lowly look from her, at best would have merited the condescending manner of a superior dealing with an inferior that *Tia* Toyang had so famously mastered.

This was the *Tia* Toyang of family lore, who was known as the Family Terror. She was truly dreadful, alarming the more fainthearted who crossed her path. With that imperious manner that came from a lifetime of having her way, she looked as though she could sweep you under the rug if you displeased her. Nonetheless, I must confess we were never particularly in awe of her. She was very often at our house, complaining to my father, complaints that became the stuff of comedy that peppered family stories. I reasoned if so much was wrong with her life, she could not rightly be a terror to me who did not have any complaint with mine. So we mostly ignored her, which secured for us a bit of approval from her, who was so used to being kowtowed to, and the menacing glance that brooked no excuses for youth's exuberance was not as alarming when turned on us.

She had a particular exasperation for *Tia* Antonina, the wife of her brother, *Tio* Nemesio, maybe because, like my mother, although not with as much sympathy, she had endured hours listening to a litany of complaints from her brother about his wife. She and *Tia* Antonina could not occupy proximate space without their dislike for each other heating up the room. Everything *Tia*

Antonina said riled *Tia* Toyang, everything *Tia* Toyang did annoyed *Tia* Antonina.

They would come to our house to complain to Father. There one of them would be on our porch, either *Tia* Toyang or *Tia* Antonina, perched on a chair, voice strident, hands gesticulating, while Father, shoulders reclined on the cushions on the couch, arms across his chest, looked and listened, most probably wishing he were somewhere else, wondering what he had done that made these women choose him to counsel them. They made him their listening post, judge, and King Solomon, whose wise patience they sorely tried.

Tia Toyang lorded it over the priests of our town as well, and she extended her reach even to the priests of the neighboring towns. The parish priest of an adjacent town had hired a woman to do housework in the convent. Apparently, she did other kinds of work, too, and when she became with child, everyone had no doubt what she did on overtime. Then she got sick and died and the parish priest, who must have felt for her as he would a true wife, laid her body in the convent. Priests from other parishes came to offer their condolence. The townspeople found this arrangement most scandalous and tongues wagged about this outrage.

One night during a wake in the convent, one priest looked out the window and saw *Tia* Toyang in full fury hurrying out of an Escaño truck. "Oh, good Lord," the priest exclaimed in panic. "It's *Señora* Toyang! It's *Señora* Toyang!"

She had brought a truckload of stones and rocks, and when she pelted the convent wall with her cargo, the priests scampered for safety, and cowered under the dining room table, away not so much from the raining rocks as from the blazing *Tia* Toyang, whose head of the blackest curls sticking out abundantly from all over her head made her look like Medusa of myth. Did she have curly hair? My sisters said no, not at all. But when stories of her imperiousness came up in family storytelling, that was how she impressed herself on my young, impressionable mind: a mythical figure with crazy hair that looked as though it had a fight with the comb, and the comb always lost.

18

The Japanese did not stay long this time. Although they had spread out and made their presence felt in the entire province of Leyte, there was no American or guerilla movement in our town as yet. In a little while, the Japanese moved out and peace reigned. During this short period of reprieve, we went on with our usual lives, the shadow of war hanging over our heads. Members of the Philippine Army came to town to organize the guerilla movement. People who had stayed away during the first Japanese occupation came back. It was a busy, tense time for the family.

Early the next year, Cristina had a baby girl. They named her Cristina, too, nicknamed her CriCri, Mother said, which I thought was a beautiful name. Since Cristina and the baby were safely ensconced with the other Lopezes in their *hacienda* in Bayabas, Juanita and Emiliana, whose concerns all along were with us and our parents, decided to come home, even though, with all the ties we had with the guerillas, they would have been safer with Cristina.

Tio Lorenzo and his family came back from Cebu, and with them Curly Coromina, and her brother, Lito, children of *Tio* Lorenzo's sister, *Tia* Paz Escaño Coromina. Curly's other brother, Ed Coromina, was already in Malitbog at this time. Ed had come and married his first cousin Nenita, *Tio* Lorenzo's daughter. Lito had fallen in love with my sister Clotilde, as had another cousin, Matoy, *Tio* Lorenzo's son. They were always together, Matoy and Lito; they were the best of friends, so that when *Tio* Lorenzo decided to move his family from Cebu to Malitbog, Lito, with not much to do in Cebu, and with romance in mind, decided to tag along with his best friend.

Tag along and fulfill his destiny.

- - - -

"Do you know what the newest song in Cebu is?" Lito asked my sisters. He and Matoy were at our house all the time. "It's called *Matud Nila.*" They Say. He proceeded to teach my sisters the song, which, like every new song they learned, filled the house for quite some time after that.

At first we would tease Clotilde. Sometimes, she would get mad and chase us, which was quite fun. Most times though, she just ignored us, ignored Lito and Matoy lounging around the house as well. Soon, it was not much fun teasing Clotilde, and we really liked Lito and Matoy, so we gave up that endeavor. She carried on with her life, efficiency personified: cleaning house, helping Mother, taking care of us, climbing coconut trees when the need to eat young coconuts moved us. How she felt for Lito nobody knew. She was too reserved, too private, still too young, and Lito was gone from our lives too soon.

Over at the villa, Emit Escaño's wife, Lolita, was having a new baby, or at least was trying to, very hard. The births of her two sons, Nene and Ramon, were agony for her---she was a small woman and the two boys entered the world strong and strapping--- but this new labor was a nightmare shared by the entire town. The baby clung to her insides and just refused to come out. War raged in other parts of the land, and although we had not felt the full extent of deprivation as yet, supplies were getting harder, if not impossible, to come by; anesthesia was just a memory, and without it, a Cesarean section was out of the question. Five doctors attended her, but without anesthesia, none of them could give her any relief.

My sisters went out each morning and came home with bulletins of Lolita's ordeal. For more than thirty hours the doctors labored over her until her husband Emit said enough.

"You have to take the baby out," Emit told Doctor Arevalo, one of the doctors in attendance.

Doctor Arevalo had ten children, six of whom would later give their lives to the service of the Church, becoming priests and nuns, and taking out a baby in a manner very like a late-term abortion was a course of action too sickening for the doctor to contemplate.

"What do you mean?" Doctor Arevalo whimpered, his face blanching painfully at the prospect. He was a slight man, cautious in manner, more tentative now with the grim-faced Emit looming larger than all the doctors in futile attendance.

"I mean take the baby out!"

"Emit, I cannot do that, you know I can't. God will be angry with me."

Catholics did not have a voice in these matters. Man might have put the baby there, but the manner of its entrance into the world was God's domain. If He willed to take back both mother and child, so be it. Man proposed, God disposed, in this very Catholic town.

But the doctors had waited too long for God to decide, and God seemed silent those days, while the husband was not, this husband who was used to having his way, through his name or his money, or his gun, which he whipped out and pointed at the doctor's head.

"Go ahead, Doctor, take that baby out," he said grimly, "I'd hate to use this, but you know I would." Years of knowing him left no doubt in everyone's mind around him that indeed he would, if he had to, maybe not fatally, but bloodily.

And so Doctor Arevalo set out to do the ghastly task of taking out a full-term baby who was tenaciously clinging to her mother's insides, without anesthesia, careful not to damage the mother too much, with the threat of a gun to his head.

All this while, people were standing by waiting for a kinder report, hoping her ordeal would end soon. There was consternation when they learned how the baby came out; there were sighs of relief when her ordeal stopped.

The doctor was just as torn. His daughter, Inday Arevalo, later recalled how he'd cried when he came home. "I did an evil thing today, I did an evil thing today," but there was not much his family could do to comfort him.

In anticipation of the return of the Japanese, the Americans arrived in town to organize the guerrilla movement. One of them was Captain Iliff David Richardson. He was a brown-haired American, not particularly tall, but with a big, wide smile that made him quite pleasant-looking. In the eyes of the people of these islands, colonized by the Spaniards for three hundred years and by the Americans for half a century after that, and fed all those years with the notion that white was more beautiful, well, one could even call him handsome.

The Americans stayed in the *Casa* while they marshaled their military resources, organized the guerilla movement and trained the men of the town for guerilla warfare. Several family members were living in the *Casa* at this time: the family of *Tio* Lorenzo, Ed Coromina and his wife, *Tio* Lorenzo's daughter Nenita, Ed's brother, Lito, and their sister, Curly.

The Corominas were noted for their brains and good looks, and the three in town, Ed, Curly, and Lito, exemplified the crop: witty, smart, fun, and extremely good looking. In no time, Curly had captivated Captain Richardson. "One cannot tire of looking at her face," he said of her.

She was an amazing woman; she was a chimney, lighting one cigarette as soon as the other went out. She could hold her drink, too, as well as any man. The lowly *tuba*, with a squeeze of lemon to disguise its strange taste, worked when no other drink was on hand. In the evenings, we would hear Curly sing *None But A Lonely Heart Can Know My Sadness*. That must have been their song, though she could not have been that sad: the *Casa* reverberated with laughter and singing until the late hours.

Several cousins, among them Otic Escaño, Emit Escaño, and Genaro Faelnar, and most of the younger men of the town, went up the mountains and joined the guerilla movement. From there they contributed to a constant flow of information to the Americans. Curly Coromina, who by this time had fallen in love with Captain Richardson, went up the mountains with him as well. An American, Ira Wolfert, later wrote a book based on Captain Richardson's story, and of the time he spent in Leyte, and indeed in Malitbog, and called it *An American Guerilla in the Philippines*. The book became the basis of the movie, which starred Tyrone Power. The people who made the movie wanted to shoot it in

Malitbog, but Ruperto Kangleon, the Secretary of Interior, denied permission. He was in the guerilla movement with Captain Richardson and witnessed first hand what happened up there in the mountains, in the *boondocks,* as the Americans called them, a word derived from the Philippine word *bundok,* for mountain, a word that would later find its way into the English language and dictionary. Ruperto Kangleon thought the book too fictionalized, glamorizing Captain Richardson into more of a hero than he really was, and he refused permission for the movie shoot. They shot the movie in another town instead.

Meanwhile, Malitbog prepared for the inevitable return of the Japanese. And return they did.

They came back with a vengeance---an army, a cavalry with artillery, and the *kempetai,* the dreaded secret police---rampaging through the town like conquerors, subjugators of the undefended, unarmed and unresisting. They occupied the garrison near our house, and again commandeered the *Casa.* This time, *Tio* Lorenzo and the other Escaños abandoned the *Casa* and moved to *Tio* Agustin's villa and to other houses in the neighboring towns. The Japanese rounded up all the men in town, confined them in the church, cooped up for days without food or water.

Mother called Ramon and me, "You have to bring food to your father. It has been some time now, he must be starving. You are just children, maybe you can take this food to the church without being noticed or harmed by the Japanese." She had packed several hard-boiled eggs, some bananas and some sweet potatoes in small packages. "Now go." We held on to the packages and off to the church we went.

Japanese soldiers guarding the church looked menacing with their bayonets. "*Kura, kura,*" one of them said, shooing us away. My brother and I crept to the side of the church looking for an entrance to get the food inside. We found a hole along a wall and since my fist was much smaller than my brother's, he told me to insert the packages inside the hole. But after putting in my hand a few times, the point of a bayonet was thrust through the hole, nearly slicing my hand. But we had a mission. We waited a few more minutes, and then I inserted another package. This time we were not hindered and we were able to put in all the packages.

After a couple of days, we heard that the Japanese had let some of the men go. Then we heard a man outside calling my mother.

"*Señora* Merced, *Señor* Dioni is coming." We hurried outside and sure enough, we saw Father trudging up the driveway. We rushed down to help him. He was very weak from the forced fasting. The next day, two Japanese officers came to our house. Father was resting on the lounge chair, looking very frail.

"We want you to drive one of our trucks for us," said the captain.

"I can't," said Father. "As you can see, I am still very weak."

The Japanese officer looked at my father, at his face peaked and pale, his hand hanging limply by his side, obviously unwell. The officer must have decided he did not want to be driven anywhere by someone as sick as that.

"Well, then, when you get better," he said.

That night, Emit, who had joined the guerrillas up in the mountains, sent down one of his men. He came in through the kitchen, and came stealthily into the dining room where we were having supper.

"*Señor* Dioni," he said, "Emit sent me down. We heard that the Japanese want you to drive their truck. You cannot do this, *Señor* Dioni," he said, "once in a while, we come down and ambush or shell any transportation that we believe are used by the Japanese. We cannot have our operations hindered by the knowledge you might be driving one of these vehicles. Please, you have to refuse."

Though Father loathed the idea of driving for the enemy, he would not have any choice if he stayed in town. "You have to go to Cebu," said Mother.

Between the devil and the deep blue sea, Father chose the latter. He sailed away one morning and stayed in Cebu until the Japanese found themselves a driver and Father was sure they would not need him. Then he came back.

19

The Japanese corralled the men left in the town to squeeze information from them about the guerilla movement. The men were tortured, and bleeding, admitted to whatever their tormentors wanted to hear, admissions that were often inaccurate, mostly fabricated. It was amazing how pain, the fear of the Japanese' reputation for cruelty, and tales of horrible methods of execution, could extract stories which before had not existed. Those who were suspected of aiding or having contact with the guerillas were imprisoned in the *Casa* and in the schoolhouse the Japanese made their temporary prison. Punishment was quick, arbitrary and, in most cases, terminal. Some, to spare themselves a fate that they knew they could not do anything about, joined the Japanese VC, a sort of volunteer constabulary. The Japanese issued them firearms and used them to guard less important points or as guides when they made their sporadic sorties into the mountains.

Where in town some traces of civilization surfaced, in the mountains foraging for Americans, the Japanese were at their most savage. As though some primal instincts for self-preservation were sharpened by the whiff of air the Americans had just breathed, by treading on soil the enemy had just trod on, the Japanese were at their most ferocious. Stories of barbaric proportions filtered down to us in the town.

On their patrol in the mountains, any person they encountered met his fate at the end of their bayonets. Fire was the Japanese' genius. They burned down fields. They burned down houses of suspected guerillas with their families still inside. They severed ears from heads, heads from bodies. *Plunder* and *pillage* became common and dreaded words.

Just when people thought that they could not come up with acts more savage, the Japanese raised their reputation for cruelty to horrifying heights.

People who accompanied them on their sorties up the mountains told of atrocities that, were they not true, a prolific writer of horror stories could not have invented. They tied children to house posts, then set the house on fire, and amidst wailing and weeping of horrified parents, watched while the house burned down to the ground, and the tied children shriveled to a crisp. They hurled babies into the air and these babies, hands wind-milling, came flying down straight onto the harrowing points of their bayonets.

-     -   -   -

One evening, we were having supper when we heard boots stomping up the stairs of our porch, then loud knocking. We looked at each other apprehensively. "It's all right," said Father reassuringly, "They just want everyone to be accounted for." He opened the door to the captain who was followed by a couple of officers and some minions.

"Good evening," said the captain. He looked at us, all standing expectantly, our hands gripping the backs of our chairs, watching them silently, wary and unwelcoming. "Go ahead and finish your supper," he said.

"We're done," said Father. "You may sit."

The captain chose the chair near the piano while his men, wooden, without expression on their faces, remained standing.

And so it started. The nightly visits, the almost-roll-calls. They always asked for every person in the house.

They came late one night and my brother and I were already asleep.

"Where are children?" the captain asked.

"It's late, they're already in bed," Father answered.

"Maybe they could be with us for a little while," the captain persevered.

Mother roused us from sleep. We came to the living room still full of sleep, rubbing our eyes with our hands, but present for inspection.

They never stayed long but they did this every night: the Japanese captain, and some officers, arriving at our house, ostensibly to talk to my father, but in reality checking each person's presence.

"They just want to make sure that none of us go to the mountains to take information to the guerillas," Father said. "Just don't volunteer information, but never tell a lie, either," he admonished us. He was very straightforward and direct in his manner, so that, although the Japanese knew that some members of our family were up in the mountains with the guerillas, they left us pretty much alone. Except for the nightly visits.

One night they came to the house and we gathered in the living room, but without Father. "Where's Stalin?" Captain Izumi asked. After so many nightly visits, he had taken a friendly attitude towards us, sometimes smiling, facetiously calling my father Stalin because of his mustache, unmindful of our always-solemn faces. He never tried to break the wall we had seriously erected around ourselves, never tried to bridge the distance of our reserve. His ease in dealing with us derived from whatever regard he had for us; he needed no response on our part.

"He's sick," Juanita replied.

"He is?" said the captain, sounding sympathetic. "Let me go see him."

"Of course," said my sister. She led him to the bedroom where Father was in bed.

"He must have doctor," the captain said. "I shall send doctor over."

The Japanese doctor came, examined Father, ascertained that he really was sick, and gave him some pills. Well, that was good, we said. Their suspicion, father's cure.

Some of our family members were swiftly rounded up. They took Lito Coromina one day, to where, we did not know. There had been a Captain Campos in the detachment that was once stationed near our town. Lito resembled Captain Campos, the Japanese said, although how, we could not understand. Captain Campos was a grown man, maybe in his forties, while Lito was just a teenager. The only resemblance we could think of was very feeble: they both looked *mestizo*, Filipinos of European or American ancestry. But the Japanese must have their man, even though it was the wrong man, and the witnesses with masks over their heads must point at somebody, even if it was the wrong somebody. It was a tragic state of affairs---people doing whatever they could to spare themselves horrendous punishment from this brutal enemy.

They also took Ed Coromina and held him in one of the rooms in the *Casa*. By this time, Ed and his wife Nenita were expecting their first child. My sisters and our other cousins would pass by the *Casa* everyday and in voices loud enough for Ed to hear, would tell stories of Nenita's condition.

"Well," they would say in very loud voices, "wasn't that the most beautiful baby girl Nenita delivered last night? Just beautiful."

"Yes, and thank God both mother and daughter are doing well. And they're naming the baby Josephine, beautiful name, don't you just think so?" They rejoiced when from one window they saw Ed's face peering through the bars. He smiled, a broad, happy smile, nodding his head, waving his hand, to let them know he'd heard. Then he mouthed, "Thanks."

My sisters and cousins did this for a few more days, broadcasting news about the family for Ed's consumption. Then one day, nobody peered out, no more smiling face, no acknowledging hand. For several days, they passed by, chattering loudly, more apprehensive than the day before. But no face appeared on that frame of a window, just the thick bars and the black space and the nothingness beyond. Ed was not there anymore. He never saw his daughter. We never saw him again.

We did not hear where they kept Lito and we worried. "Let me see what I can do," said Vicente, our houseboy. He went around town whistling *Matud Nila*. First he passed by the Casa, whistling the tune. If Lito was there, he would surely know that it was somebody from our house. But Vicente got no response. Then he sauntered past the schoolhouse, still whistling the song. Sure enough, Lito's face emerged behind the window bars. When he saw Vicente, he moved his hand to his mouth. He's hungry, thought Vicente. He motioned for Lito to wait, and raced back to the house and to Mother.

"*Senora* Merced, *Senora* Merced," he gasped, trying to catch his breath. "He's at the schoolhouse, Lito's at the schoolhouse. And he's hungry."

My mother and sisters bustled about, securely wrapping in a piece of cloth some bananas and sweet potatoes, the only food we had in the house. Vicente hurried back to the schoolhouse with some women neighbors. Again he whistled Lito's song, and again Lito appeared at the window. The women engaged the Japanese guards in conversation, laughing, giggling, flirting with them, while under the window, Vicente jumped up and down like a child on a trampoline, until he got the package of food through to Lito.

They did this for a few days, my mother and my sisters packing food, Vicente whistling *Matud Nila*. Then one day Lito did not appear at the window. He never appeared again; that was the last we heard of him, until the end of the war when we learned of the horrendous way he must have died.

For being the wife of Emit Escaño, whom everyone knew was active in the guerilla movement up in the mountains, the Japanese took Lolita from the villa and held her prisoner in the *Casa*. She was allowed crumbs of privileges: she could receive food from outside; she could send her clothes to the villa to be laundered. She inserted notes inside the hem of her dresses and *Tio* Agustin tried to send her the things she asked for.

With Emit in the mountains and Lolita in the nether regions of the *Casa, Tio* Agustin became mother and father and grandfather to Lolita's two sons, Nene and Ramon, as well as an overwhelmed father-in-law to Lolita. Much later, with peace restored to our lives, we discovered Lolita's notes among *Tio* Agustin's things. She would ask for news of the children, for fruits and other foodstuffs. After the war ended, the family dug up all the conceivable spaces behind the Casa where she could have been buried, but they never found her body.

20

Strangely, my most vivid recollection of this time of war was hunger, not fear. My father was there, a rock who would shield us from the Japanese. But the hunger never seemed to leave me. Before the Japanese stopped all travel in and out of the town, Mother brought back from our farm some thirty sacks of rice, just in time before travel was prohibited. We then had several sacks of rice sitting in our warehouse. But Father was not sure how long the war was going to last. Since several people were staying in our house at all times, Father started us on rations, rice porridge for breakfast and supper, and regular rice only for lunch. But rice was supposed to be eaten with *something,* and that something we did not have.

Everybody started to plant *camote,* sweet potatoes, along the sidewalks of town. Ramon planted a patch of about five square meters in Mother's flower garden which gave us not only good *camote* but also good new vine shoots that we ate as vegetables or salad. These were just leaves, and after being on the menu for months on end, they really began to taste like leaves. Sometimes, to extend the rice a bit, Mother would mix the porridge with *camote,* but long before the next meal rolled around, I would be hungry again.

We were encapsulated in the town; nobody from outside was allowed to enter, and nobody from inside to leave. Those who left town were suspected of having guerilla connections and were tortured when they came back, so that those who stayed, stayed, and those who left, left for good.

- -   -   -

Once in a while, Japanese cargo ships delivered supplies to the Japanese soldiers in the Casa and in the garrison near our house.

We would watch for these Japanese ships and when we saw that one had docked at the wharf, my brother and I would run over to the pier and unobtrusively wait nearby as Japanese soldiers unloaded sacks of dried fish and rice. These shipments were precious to my brother and me, and a welcome source of extra food for our family.

They were old stuff, though. The sacks had sprouted holes in transport: when the soldiers plunked the sacks down on the ground, part of their contents would spill out of the holes. My brother and I would wait until the Japanese left. Then we would come out of our hiding place, gather the rice and the dried fish on the ground, sift off and clean the earth from them. Work on the rice was slow and hard, the stones were hardly larger than the grains we separated them from.

"Hurry," Ramon urged on one such night when we were working on our pickings, "it's getting dark." Night had fallen by the time we were done. This time, our cache was meager. Other times, when the sacks were really old, or when the Japanese soldiers were more impatient and dumped the sacks harder on the ground, the sacks ripped bigger holes and our hoard would be more plentiful. Sadly, tonight we were not so lucky. Still, we brought home what little we collected proudly to our mother. She cooked the dried fish with the *camote* leaves. Supper that night was at least a change.

Most times, we subsisted on everything cooked with coconut milk---leaves with coconut milk, bananas with coconut milk, everything with coconut milk that to this day, I cannot *look* at, much less eat, anything with that white stuff in it.

Most of the time, aside from ourselves, as many as four families were living in our house, cousins, or families of my father's friends, who were stranded in the town, or who evacuated to our town from the city when the war broke out. Father divided whatever food we had equally among so many. I never knew how Father managed to survive on so little, big man that he was, when most times he even shared *his* share with Mother and with us. Even so, there was never enough, and the hunger was a grief that never left me.

Emit's real father, *Señor* Emilio Javier, and Emit's brother, Alfredo Javier, went up the mountains to join the guerillas. Alfredo's wife, Paquita, later followed, leaving behind Alfredo's mother, *Señora* Cleta, with his three small children. One day, Father was walking to church and saw *Señora* Cleta and her grandchildren sitting by the side of the road.

"Cleta, what are you doing here?" asked Father, looking at the children.

"Oh, Dioni, we don't have anywhere to go."

Emit Escaño was adopted by *Tio* Agustin, but everyone in town knew that he was a Javier and *Señora* Cleta's son. Lest they exacerbate the Japanese' hostility to those who had connections with the guerillas, other family members were naturally wary of taking them in.

"Why don't you and the children stay in our house," said Father. "Come." Our house was already teeming, but there was a war, they needed a place to stay. And so they came and stayed at our house, too.

At one time, two daughters of *Señor* Toñing Cruz, Father's friend, stayed at our house with their husbands, having fled Cebu: Nena and Johnny Paradiez, and Nenita and Badong Abiera. Father put the four of them in the guest room, a corner room facing the gardens in front and the trees on the side of the house. Often during the day, they would close the door of their bedroom.

"Do you sometimes wonder why they often close their bedroom door?" I asked my brother. He was lounging on top of a tree and I followed in his wake.

"When their bedroom door is closed, it means that they are eating inside," Ramon answered.

"Eating what," I asked.

"Their own food," he answered.

"How do you know?" I asked.

"Because I saw them," he accentuated each syllable, looking smug. He was always on top of one fruit tree or another, where he could see into the bedrooms of the house.

"How could they eat their own food and share ours, too?" I asked. To that he did not have an answer.

Anyway, little could be hidden from Ramon. When adults converged and conversed, he hovered, placed himself strategically at hearing distances, listening. I have this fond memory of my brother, then younger and still shorter, skipping and bounding, looking up eagerly at our older cousins as they walked and talked, matching their long strides with his shorter ones, trying hard to listen to whatever it was they were talking about. He was, therefore, privy to secrets that were not intended for our young ears, and was a good source of gossip about what was going on in the house, in the family, in the town.

Sometimes, the adults became aware of Ramon's presence nearby. "*Hay Moros en la costa*," they would warn, as did the ancient Spaniards when they spied the dreaded Moors within harming distance. Sometimes, though, the battle cry came too late; the tirade of gossip had already poured out of their lips before they noticed Ramon within hearing distance.

"Ramon," Badong Abiera said, "we don't want you to repeat what you heard here, do you understand?"

"Yes," said my brother.

"Don't forget now, don't say anything," Badong repeated.

"Yes," said my brother.

"Careful now, you might forget and say something." How a grown man could nag so!

"I said I won't," my brother said loudly, exasperated.

Later of course, he would forget what it was he was not supposed to repeat.

-    -   -   -

When I was not with my brother, I immersed myself in the solitude of my own world, a world where hunger was not the overriding concern. To take my mind off the gnawing in my stomach that refused to go away, I fashioned figures from my imagination with a small knife that I tied around my waist with a piece of string, guerrilla style, and these served me well into journeys my heart longed to take me. A stalk of a banana plant, with the leaf shaped like a horse's head, carried me off to other lands, another world before this, when abundance flowed through my careless hands and I did not think to hoard. I'd ride the stalk with the wind, off to other lands flowing with food, leaving behind a small, often-empty stomach.

Ramon, always more enterprising and down to earth, raised a few chickens, which became his friends. But even his chickens felt the weight of war. Most of them died of chicken disease and those that survived had spindly bodies and did not produce many eggs. It was a frustrating enterprise to raise our own foodstuff, anyway. What food the Japanese saw, they fancied, and what they fancied, they bought, with Japanese money which could not buy anything since there was nothing to buy. But we did not have any say in these matters.

Emiliana, down to a scrawny eighty-something pounds, concerned my parents.

"You have to eat," Father would coax.

But she could not take all the rice porridge that was the only food we had for stretches of time. She would chew and chew the spoonful in her mouth but still could not bring it down.

Ramon was stroking the feathers of his chicken when Father came down and sat beside him.

"We have to do something for your sister," said Father to Ramon, eyeing the chicken Ramon was fondling.

"No, Papa, no," Ramon protested tearfully.

"Would you rather the chicken lives and your sister doesn't?" The chicken became *arroz con pollo* for supper, chicken boiled with lots of rice. Ramon did not even sit down at table, which was a mercy. He did not see me devour his friend.

-    -   -   -

A Japanese lieutenant came to our house one windy afternoon, alone. He was one of the minor officers who would come to the house in the early evenings with the captain and other soldiers, so coming alone, in the middle of the afternoon, was a chilling change. We gathered in the living room, silently watching him.

"I just want to borrow this little one here," he said. He looked at me and said, "Come with me to the house." Seeing the consternation on everyone's face, he said, "It's all right, just for a visit."

Father said that this officer was different from the other Japanese in our town. He was less brusque in his manner and speech, seemed more educated. If one could call an adversary with a reputation for cruelty a gentleman, one could call him that, too, but even though he treated us with more respect than did the other men in his command, he was not someone we should be having conversations with. And he was still the enemy. Father's brows knitted with worry.

We followed the lieutenant down the porch steps, Father holding my hand, the rest of the family following quickly behind us. "Just tell the truth when he asks questions," Father said. He put his hand on my shoulder reassuringly, "and there is nothing to fear."

I bounded after the lieutenant to the *Casa,* up the stairs to his bedroom. It was a sparse room for an officer, nothing but a bed, a table, a couple of chairs, and pictures on top of the desk. I wondered what happened to the other pieces of furniture that used to be here.

Father did not have to worry about me. The time I spent with the lieutenant in the *Casa* was his time, and he did the talking while I did the listening. He had children my age, he said. He went to the desk on the other side of the room and picked up a frame. In it was a picture of a boy and a girl.

"That's my daughter, and my son. He's as big as you, as tall," he said wistfully. "How old are you?"

"Nine." I looked at the picture. "He looks like you," I said. This made him smile.

"They were good in school," he said. "Were you good in school?"

"Yes," I said. "I'm good at numbers," I added.

"You are? Are you good with your Tables? How much is eight times eight?"

"Sixty-four," I answered quickly. I almost laughed out loud. That was easy.

"Good," he said, smiling. "Open your hand." He placed a couple of cookies on my palm. Cookies! I was very, very thankful, and told him so. I picked one up and put it in my mouth, breathing in its smell deeply, waiting for my taste buds to spring awake as they became aware that these were no longer leaves inside my mouth. I let it rest on my tongue, savoring it slowly until it softened completely and I had to swallow it. Jeez, that was good! I would recite to him the entire multiplication table if I could get more cookies for that.

"Do you want me to recite the whole multiplication table to you?" I asked eagerly.

"You know the entire Table?" he asked. A very amused smile spread on his face, crinkling his eyes to slits, wiping off the serious expression that was always pasted on his face.

"I do," I said promptly. I opened my mouth and was about to start but he tapped me on the shoulder.

"I believe you, I believe you," he laughed. It was a very pleasant laugh, a gurgling sound from deep inside him, one I never would have associated with him. "Here, open your hand." He took the last couple of cookies from the container on the desk and put them on my open palm. He nodded at me and put his hand lightly on my head. I picked up bits of cookies from my hand while I listened to him talk.

"He must miss his family," I later told Father.

"You'll be all right," said Father.

- - - -

The Japanese, too, were beginning to feel the deprivation of war. Food was just as scarce for them as it was for us. One day, Nenita Abiera was in the kitchen, frying a piece of chicken. Where she got that small piece we never knew. The chicken done, she went to the dining room to fetch a plate. When she came back to the kitchen, she saw this small Japanese soldier creeping towards the stove. He must have come to the house with some orders from above when he had a whiff of the chicken frying in the kitchen. He was about to snatch Nenita's fried chicken! But there was no way Nenita was giving up this coveted treasure. She took two huge steps, grabbed the frying pan, tossed the chicken into the plate, and started hitting the frying pan on the poor fellow's head.

"How dare you steal my chicken!" The Japanese raced down the kitchen stairs, with Nenita in hot pursuit, still pounding the frying pan on his head, with the hapless man running and covering his head with his hands, fleeing as though the devil himself, or a horde of Americans, was snapping at his heels.

-    -   -   -

Seeing how crowded we were in our house, *Tia* Piling offered Nena and Nenita and their husbands Johnny Paradiez and Badong Abiera, a house that was owned by her family, which was empty at the moment. The two couples moved from our house to *Tia* Piling's house.

Ramon went over to see how they fared in their new place. On the way up, he saw Johnny's bike leaning against the wall outside, with a box tied to the back.

"Johnny Apricots," Ramon said, reading the words on the box. Johnny had written his name on top of the box label that read *Apricots*.

"What did you say?" Johnny asked.

"Johnny Apricots," said my brother, very seriously, pointing a forefinger to the letters on the box, "it says right here on the box."

Perceiving insult where only mischief stirred, Johnny ordered Ramon out of *Tia* Piling's house. "Leave my house this minute," he said.

Of course this story was told and retold, with much amusement. *And it was not even his house!* That's how Johnny was called thereafter, long after the war ended, when family members converged and recalled stories of the war, *Johnny Apricots,* compliments of my brother Ramon.

-    -   -   -

The war had dragged on for such a long time and our relatives up in the mountains were concerned that we had nothing left to eat. One day a farmer came to our house. He said that he came from the mountains, with something from Emit. He extended his hand, showing us a bamboo pole he was carrying. They had hallowed out the inside of the pole. There, carefully wrapped, they had hidden some salted fish.

"Tell Emit we are thankful, but tell him not to send us anything again. Contact with us in any way could mean death for us if we are found out," Father told the farmer.

We were interned in the town; we could not even avail of food from out of it.

-    -   -   -

To assuage their hunger, the Japanese turned to the sea. The fastest way to fish was to use hand grenades and this they did sometimes. When we saw them preparing to do this, we would hide under the pier. They would motor their boat to the sea, throw in the grenade and the explosion sent a spray of fish bursting out of the water. We waited until they had gathered their harvest and gone home. Then we would forage for the remaining fish that they left behind, floating there belly up, stunned by the explosion. Fish thrived in the deeper, farther waters, which could have eased the town's hunger, but we were not allowed to have boats, or any means of serious transport, that might take us out of town. The Japanese posted sentries in front of the *Casa*, which looked unto the sea, at all hours of night and day, guns at the ready, and nobody could venture too far out into the sea. And so hunger came to our town to visit, and stayed, and stayed.

21

A river flowed at the back of our house. Sometimes, when it rained hard and long, the water rose, snaking under the wood bridge that spanned it, swallowing filth as it dashed along the way, and disgorging its catch into the sea, a cleansing rush that cleared its path of flotsam and debris. As the weather cleared, so would the river, and the Japanese came down in their G-strings to do their wash.

This was laundry time! My brother and I raced through the trees at the back of our house and slipped down to the river. Two Japanese soldiers emerged from the path outside the fence that surrounded our house, balancing between their scrawny arms a container which held their laundry, their slippers flip-flopping against the stones, looking very naked, with just their G-strings on.

"Wash your clothes?" we offered. They contemplated us, wondering how good a washing job children could do. But the prospect of idling about while someone else washed their clothes was a temptation too hard to resist.

"Okay."

It was not very hard work. Exceptionally clean laundry was not expected. The river ran clear and fast as it rushed over stones on its way to the sea. After we soaped the clothes, we spread them out and the current, surging swiftly that it bent the grasses that lined the edges of the river, washed away the soap from the clothes. A little squeezing and twisting after that and we were done.

While we washed their clothes, they took off their G-strings and washed them themselves, squatting naked on the edge of the river. We almost choked trying to check our laughter as we saw their uncircumcised penises hanging between their legs. Uncircumcised, Jeez! We had to endure so much pain and embarrassment when we had to go through the wretched ordeal ourselves, felt the pain even before the actual pain manifested itself. We walked around the house wide-legged as cowboys, stepping gingerly lest our injured staffs touch the cloth wrapped around our middles and waken the nerves that were resting from the distressing incident they had just suffered through!

Well, at least they washed their own underwear themselves, although I never knew whether they considered G-strings underwear; often they could be seen walking around with nothing on but those thongs barely covering their private parts.

We were done. We had rinsed out as much of the soap as we could. We carried the wash in our arms, still dripping wet. My small hands could not squeeze out all the water from the clothes and my already damp shirt was getting more soaked. I felt the sweat on my brow starting to trickle down my face, making my nose itch. I dumped our load on a large rock in front of the Japanese, and rubbed the itch out of my nose.

"There," we announced.

"You can keep the soap," they said. We were careful not to scrub too hard and the bars were still thick and fat. This was the payment we expected for services rendered. We ran back to the house and happily gave the soap to our mother.

Soap, another necessity so hard to come by, and so mothered inventions. Roque, *Tio* Lorenzo's son, tried his hand at soap making, using what crude materials he could get. Coconut oil he could get. We did not know what else he used, that was his trade secret. He polished his handiwork until the soap came out passable enough for use, making abundant lather; then he went about marketing it, using soap for barter.

-   -   -   -

With so many people staying in our house, the four bedrooms upstairs were not enough, large though they were, and Father converted another room downstairs for us.

One early evening, when most everyone in town was inside preparing for the night, my brother and I heard sounds coming from outside our house, sounds like feet scuffling against dry ground. Our house stood on a corner land surrounded by walls of cement, high enough to keep outsiders out, but not too high, so that from our windows we could see outside the fence. At one side of our house, a footpath led from the road to the river at the back of our house. It was a narrow path, bordered by a few short shrubs and weeds and some sorry vegetations.

On this evening, my brother and I were very curious when we heard these sounds outside. We stood at the side of the window looking out, trying to make ourselves as inconspicuous as we could. The sun had faded on the trees outside and shadows had fallen from a sky of gray. There was still light enough to see but not bright enough to broadcast anyone's passage.

We saw men with their hands tied behind their backs being herded like cattle along the path by Japanese soldiers, the points of their bayonets prodding the men's backs. We crouched motionless by the window, not knowing what would happen, but certain that something evil was coming our way. When they went past our view, we sprinted upstairs and looked out the dining room window where we could see the river. The men and the soldiers splashed their way across the low water to the other side. By now, it was too dark to see across the river through the trees. We went back to our bedroom and waited. After a long while, the Japanese soldiers came back up the path, wiping their bayonets with their shirts. The men were nowhere in sight. We found this very upsetting, and frightening, too, but this ritual hypnotized us, pasted us to the window like glue.

We witnessed this same ritual many, many times. We knew we were witnesses to something horrible, but could not tear ourselves away from the window. In these early evenings, at the first hint of night falling, as soon as we heard those footsteps outside our house, we would creep stealthily to our posts, peer out at the dirt road outside, as still as mice, lest our parents notice what we were doing, give us a scolding, and send us to bed. We looked forward to witnessing this ceremony almost every night, with trepidation, most certainly, but with excitement as well.

During the dry season, the river would shrink and one could walk knee-deep in water across to the piece of land on the other side. It was an eerie place, always wind-blown, scrubby with weeds, planted with a few coconut trees, and was almost always deserted. Other people must have seen what we saw on that dirt path outside our house, most certainly must have talked about what happened on that footpath on those frightful evenings. When the war ended, people dug up that stretch of land, looking for missing family members that the Japanese had taken away from their homes. They came up with severed body parts, pieces of bones scattered under the earth, that at one time belonged to their family members, and to put a closure to this terrible time, so they hoped.

22

Battle of Leyte Gulf – October 23 – 26, 1944

There was much excitement that night.

We were at table, just starting dinner, when we heard rumblings, as though of thunder pummeling the sky.

"What was that?" said Father, putting down the fork with which he was about to spear a piece of food from his plate. Then we heard it again: explosions of what seemed like fireworks, the rat-tat-tat of machine guns, the ping-ping sound of guns.

"Let me go and see what's happening," said Father. He drank his water hastily, rose from the table and hurried out of the house. We left the table, too, and followed him. People were running down the street to the shore. We found Father standing on the pier, looking towards the sea. By this time, the pier was getting crowded, with people crowding about.

It was a clear night and from the wharf where we stood, we could see Panaon Island across the bay, an angry orange spectacle hanging over it in an otherwise dark blue sky. We saw what looked like an exhibition of fireworks, and heard explosions of gunfire. Patrol Torpedo (PT) boats raced through the waters, crosscutting around jets of water bursting from the sea. Searchlights flashed, tracer bullets crisscrossed the night sky, and traversed the horizon. Sprays of fireworks cascaded from the evening sky. Lights from explosions illuminated the sea, and we could see the smaller PT boats seemingly chasing the larger ships. When bombs exploded in the water, great geysers of water spurted from the sea, soared up to the sky and ended in graceful sprays. Sounds like thunder rumbled through the din. The rattle of machine gun was everywhere and aircraft screeched as they plunged from the sky. Lights streaked like meteors showers; colored bursts of smoke added to the display.

Thus, we stood on the pier, and without being aware of it, watched the night battle between the Japanese and American forces, and witnessed the beginnings of the greatest naval battle ever fought: the Battle of Leyte Gulf. And history. Thus was opened for me the path to an enduring interest in times past, and the Second World War especially, that lasted all my life.

-     -   -   -

"The greatest of all naval battles" it was indeed, that history would later teach us. Everything about this battle was described in the superlative---the largest battleships, the largest warships in the world, actually the largest ever built (the *Yamato* and *Musashi*), the larger-than life General Douglas MacArthur. More than 282 American, Australian and Japanese ships were involved, two hundred thousand men participated, with an impressive cast that included President Franklin Delano Roosevelt, General Douglas MacArthur, Admiral Chester Nimitz, Admiral William "Bull" Halsey, Jr., Vice Admiral Thomas Kinkaid, Admiral Takeo Kurita, names that directed the course of that dark, terrible time in the history of mankind.

-     -   -   -

This history began in 1942, in those early days of the war when defeat followed defeat for the Allies. In March, the British surrendered in Singapore, the Dutch surrendered to the Japanese in Java, and President Roosevelt ordered that most famous of his generals, General Douglas MacArthur, to leave the Philippines. This was the general the American people had put to a pedestal. Women were naming their babies after him, universities were conferring honorary degrees on him. It would not do to have the Japanese capture him and hang him in a public square. Standing aboard a 77-foot PT boat, General MacArthur uttered his now historic pledge, "I shall return," and escaped to Australia, leaving behind a combined, bereft American-Filipino contingent of some 80,000.

A month later, in April, the infamous Bataan Death March began: some 76,000 Allied Prisoners of War, including 12,000 Americans, were forced to walk to a new Prisoner-of-War camp sixty miles away under the blazing tropical sun. Prisoners were deliberately refused food or water, hit with the butt of rifles when they became too weak to go on, gored with bayonets when no force on earth could raise them up from the ground on where they fell. Japanese trucks drove over bodies of those who fell; Japanese in vehicles indifferently stuck out their bayonets and cut throats of men marching along the road. There were reports of rampant beheadings, disembowelments and rape, even of civilians who attempted to help the prisoners. Post war reports placed the death toll between five to eleven thousand men and estimated that only 54,000 of the 76,000 prisoners reached the Prisoner-of-War camp.

In May, the Japanese captured Manila and the US Naval Base in Cavite, General Wainwright surrendered unconditionally all US and Filipino forces, the Japanese took Corregidor, and the Philippines fell.

Now, some two years after the fall of Bataan, the Allied forces began the reconquest of the Philippines. Japanese intelligence intercepted a message that General MacArthur, with a formidable force, was planning to invade Leyte. The Japanese made an all-out preparation to stop this invasion. The Japanese could ill afford to lose Leyte as it stood in the heart of their supply lines. With the Americans in control of Leyte, Japanese traffic lanes of rubber, precious oil, and reinforcement would be cut off. The loss of the Philippines would be tantamount to losing the war. The Japanese navy, therefore, concentrated their effort to crush the invasion.

Preparations for the Battle for Leyte began.

Under General Douglas MacArthur's Southwest Pacific Forces, the Seventh Fleet, commanded by Vice Admiral Thomas Kinkaid, would provide naval support to MacArthur's Forces.

Under Admiral Chester Nimitz' Central Pacific Command, Admiral William "Bull" Halsey, Jr., was appointed Commander of the American Third Fleet, at this time the strongest part of the American Naval forces and the most powerful fleet to roam the seas in World War II. Task Force 38, under the command of Vice Admiral Marc Mitscher, was created to provide support to Admiral Halsey's Third Fleet. It consisted of a flagship, aircraft carriers, light aircraft carriers and a mass of supporting ships in preparation for the landings on Leyte.

The Third Fleet would defend San Bernardino Strait against any incursions by the Japanese on its way to Leyte Gulf.

The Seventh Fleet would guard Surigao Strait.

Through intelligence reports, the Japanese were well aware of the large amphibious fleet that was spearheading the invasion (Kinkaid's Seventh). They were also aware of Halsey's enormous force ready to lend support. Against these two formidable forces, the Japanese knew the obstacles they had to overcome to come up on top of this engagement.

Unless they devised a plan. They would put up a force as a decoy that would lure part of the American forces away from Leyte Gulf.

The Japanese planned a three-pronged attack.

The Southern Force, consisting of two groups--Rear Admiral Nashimura's force with two battleships, *Fuso* and *Yamashiro*, one heavy cruiser, *Mogami* and four destroyers, and Admiral Shima's with three cruisers and four destroyers--would enter through Surigao Strait into Leyte Gulf.

The Center Force, the more powerful of the battleship forces, with five battleships, ten heavy cruisers, two light cruisers and fifteen destroyers, under the command of the top Japanese Naval Commander Vice Admiral Kurita, would penetrate through San Bernardino Strait, then steam through the coast of Samar. The forces would meet up inside Leyte Gulf and attack the American landing forces there. The Center Force fleet included the *Yamato* and *Musashi,* the largest warships ever built, with their 18.1-inch guns larger than the 16-inch of the largest battleships of the United States Navy.

The Northern Force, under Vice Admiral Ozawa, with several aircraft carriers, cruisers, destroyers, and destroyer escorts, would serve as decoy to lure Admiral Halsey far away to the north, hopefully leaving San Bernardino Strait unprotected, and Kurita's formidable Center Force to pass through unimpeded, and thus engage the American invasion force of battleships, cruisers and destroyers at Leyte Gulf.

"Bull" Halsey was not only one of the US Navy's most controversial admirals; he certainly was one of its most colorful, with his flamboyant style and equally flamboyant pronouncements. Upon hearing a Japanese radio broadcast mockingly asking, "Where is the American Navy?" Halsey directed an aide, "Send them our longitude and altitude." Surveying the destruction the Japanese had wrought in Pearl Harbor, he roared, "Before we're through with them, the Japanese language will be spoken only in hell." And what Navy man at that time had not heard his exhortation, "Kill Japs! Kill Japs! Kill more Japs!"

He was aggressive, a risk-taker, a leader with a forceful personality, but hardly an intellectual. He charged with his heart more often than with his head.

On the afternoon of the October 24, 1944, Halsey's Helldivers located the carriers of Vice Admiral Ozawa's decoy Northern Force. Determined to crush Ozawa's fleet, Halsey moved all his available strength swiftly to the north to annihilate the Japanese carrier force. Halsey had swallowed Ozawa's bait, hook, line and sinker. He dashed off with his *entire* force, leaving not so much as a picket destroyer to guard San Bernardino. True to the Japanese plan, this left San Bernardino wide open for Kurita's fleet to enter Leyte unopposed. In his haste to crush Ozawa's fleet, Halsey did not even notify Kinkaid and his Seventh Fleet that they were not now being protected by the Third Fleet.

The Seventh Fleet earlier had intercepted a signal from Halsey that Task Force 34 was being formed. To Kinkaid and his staff, it was beyond imagination that Halsey would leave San Bernardino Strait unprotected. They therefore presumed that Task Force 34 had already been formed to guard the Strait, unaware that Task Force 34 had in fact *not yet* been formed and that the ships that were supposed to compose Task Force 34 had all steamed north to join Halsey's Third Fleet in its pursuit of Ozawa's decoy fleet.

Confident that Halsey would take care of Kurita's Center Force, Kinkaid and the Seventh Fleet went on its way to engage Nashimura and Shima's Southern Force in Surigao Strait.

Rear Admiral Jesse Olendorf was charged with stopping the Southern Force. With battleships, remnants of Pearl Harbor, heavy and light cruisers, destroyers and PT boats, Olendorf steamed into Surigao Strait, ready to do battle with the Southern Force.

For more than three hours, the PT boats attacked Nashimura's force, crippling Nashimura's two battleships: *Fuso* and *Yamashiro*. *Fuso* exploded and broke in two. *Yamashiro*, unaware of *Fuso*'s demise, lumbered along, straight into the second group of US destroyers, opening herself as a torpedo ripped into her. Approaching Leyte Gulf, *Yamashiro* neared the narrows where Olendorf had gathered his battleships. Behind a screen of cruisers, Olendorf's battleships opened fire on *Yamashiro*. Nashimura realized that no help was forthcoming from *Fuso* and he was not likely to survive this overpowering onslaught of Olendorf's guns. *Yamashiro* turned around and torpedoes from the destroyer *Newcomb* finished her off: *Yamashiro*, with Nashimura on board, turned over and sank in the strait.

Following Nashimura's fleet, Rear Admiral Shima's "Second Striking Force" approached Surigao Strait and quickly came under attack from the PT boats. Seeing the two halves of *Fuso*, which he thought were the wrecks of Nashimura's battleships, Shima saw no sense in plodding forward, and ordered his ships to retire. Two survivors of Nashimura's force followed: the destroyer *Shigure*, and the cruiser *Mogami*. Shima's flagship *Nachi,* misjudging *Mogami*'s speed, vainly tried to avoid a collision; too late, *Mogami*'s bow plunged into *Nachi*'s stern. *Nachi* was able to detach herself, but *Mogami*, with her steering room heavily flooded, fell behind. Too slow to escape Olendorf's screen, they shelled her until she was rendered immobile. She was sunk by aircraft the following morning.

The Battle of Surigao Strait was the last battleship-versus-battleship action in history.

The Seventh Fleet had a task group of eighteen escort carriers, divided into three task units of six carriers each. These units were referred to by their radio call-signs as Taffy One, Taffy Two and Taffy Three. Taffy One and Taffy Two were on a mission to support the American GIs who earlier had gone ashore at Leyte Gulf. Taffy Three, under the command of Rear Admiral Clifton "Ziggy" Sprague, had the task of covering the ships in Leyte Gulf.

Admiral Kurita's Center Force, with five battleships, seven heavy and two light cruisers, and thirteen destroyers steamed into San Bernardino Strait, prepared to do battle, and found the Strait empty of American force. The only impediment that stood between Kurita's Center Force and the American beachhead at Leyte Gulf was Admiral Sprague's Taffy Three, with six escort carriers, each with 25 aircraft, three destroyers (DDs), three destroyer escorts (DEs) and their 5-inch guns, a miniature fighting force when compared to Kurita's behemoth Center Force.

On his part, mistakenly thinking that he had run into Halsey's Third Fleet, Kurita ordered his ships into pursuit formation. This order caused confusion within the Japanese formation.

Taffy Three was not overly concerned. The threat of the Southern Force had been eradicated by Olendorf the night before, and Halsey's Third Fleet with its enormous strength was there guarding San Bernardino Strait, or so Clifton Sprague of Taffy Three and his men erroneously thought. Minutes later, Taffy Three was under fire. Heavy shells started pouring on them. Clifton Sprague knew he was in deep trouble. He turned his carriers east at great speed, ordered his ships to make smokescreen, and launched all his aircraft.

Sprague then ordered his destroyers Hoel, Hermann and Johnston to counterattack. The three destroyer escorts followed with their 5-inch guns. The Japanese battleship fired on Hoel, shattering her bridge. Hoel nevertheless launched her torpedoes which, although they all missed, forced Kurita's battleship to turn violently, splintering out of formation, causing confusion in the Japanese formation. Heavy shells battered Hoel, damaging her port engines and turrets. Still the shattered Hoel fired more torpedoes. One gunner, with his middle split open, tried to keep his intestines from spilling out with one hand while the other hand fired Hoel's last guns. Heavily hit, Hoel went down, bringing 253 of her crew to their watery graves.

Hermann and Johnston did not leave the fray, launched torpedoes, and attacked. Sprague's three destroyers engaged Kurita's heavy ships and forced the flagship Yamato to turn away. It never got back into action. Hoel and Johnston were sunk, but they caused so much confusion that Kurita never regained control of the Center Force.

This gallantry and bravery stunned Kurita. If this was just part of the Third Fleet, Kurita must have reasoned, and the rest of Halsey's fleet was still coming, what chance did his men have of coming out alive.

Vice Admiral Takeo Kurita, the top Japanese naval commander, was all too human after all. Wanting to avoid any more fatalities, daunted by the show of heroism shown by the men of Taffy Three, and construing wrongly that the ships in front of him were part of the formidable Third Fleet that might already be on its way towards his location and it was just a matter of time before it would start annihilating his already depleted force, failed to realize that this was not the Seventh Fleet, covered by the Third Fleet. Unaware that he had the upper hand, that if he forged on *he* could annihilate the severely overpowered American force, that he could win the engagement over this heavily crippled and orphaned opponent, Admiral Takeo Kurita turned around and ordered his fleet home.

With this turn of events, the sands of the Japanese Imperial Navy started to run out.

These engagements were amazingly riddled with errors. An American cruiser, mistaking one of its own for an enemy ship, fired on one side, the Japanese fired on the other, putting the destroyer *USS Albert W. Grant* in a mortal crossfire. Hit on all sides by friend and foe, it went down. There were jumbled messages, misunderstood communications, all astonishing, given that this engagement was headed by the best generals the two countries could offer.

With Leyte secured, General Douglas MacArthur, amidst flourish and fanfare, splashed down the shores of Leyte in his triumphant return and proclaimed: "People of the Philippines, I have returned...."

Admiral Yonai, the Japanese Navy Minister, said that "the defeat at Leyte was tantamount to the loss of the Philippines."

Historians called it the naval battle instrumental in bringing about the end of World War II. The outcome might have been entirely different. But despite the miscommunications, despite the monumental blunders, despite the incomprehensible errors, the Americans prevailed. As Admiral Clifton Sprague wrote: "The failure of the enemy . . . to wipe out all vessels of this task unit can be attributed to our successful smoke screen, our torpedo counterattack, continuous harassment of the enemy, bomb, torpedo and strafing air attacks, and the definite partiality of Almighty God."

23

A few days after that, we received from Emit and other relatives from the mountains two copies of the magazine *Free Philippines*. Afraid that the Japanese would discover the magazines in our house, my sisters hid them under the skirt of Santa Filomena, the statue on the altar in their room, carefully wrapping the magazines around the statue's legs. They waited until nighttime. Then by the light of a small kerosene lamp, they would stay down on the floor and eagerly read the magazines. Hence we knew that liberation was not very far off.

- -   -   -

For a time after that we did not have any news from the mountains. Then one day a messenger disguised as a farmer came to see Father with an urgent message from Emit. He wanted to see Father at the earliest possible opportunity at the beach near the town cemetery.

Father agreed to meet him a week later at noon. Father secured a small boat from one of the fishermen in our neighborhood. Together with Juanita, he went out to sea the next day. So as not to invite attention and suspicion, they pretended to go fishing right in front of the Casa, where the Japanese were staying. Every day after that, they would go a little farther along the shore towards the cemetery. On the agreed-upon day, Father went alone, pretending to fish right in front of the Casa but slowly inching towards the meeting place, where he met the messenger from Emit.

"I was instructed to tell you that the Americans are coming. When they come they are going to strafe the town. You must leave town as soon as possible."

"Do you have a definite date when they want us to leave?" Father asked.

"Emit said as soon as possible."

"I need another week, tell Emit that. I have to notify Agustin and Lorenzo in the villa, and the family of Jacinto, too."

"Well, I shall tell Emit that. I'm sure a week is all right. You must leave at night so as not to arouse the suspicions of the Japanese. Meanwhile, look for places up the mountains where you could stay until this is over. You must synchronize your departure and leave town simultaneously. Be very discreet. And very, very careful."

Father went to the villa to relay the message to *Tio* Agustin and *Tio* Lorenzo. Then he went to the house of Jacinto Aberásturi. They set a date and hour for the evacuation. They all agreed that each family would look for its own place to stay. There was no one place large enough to accommodate all of us.

The week gave Mother time to go out and look for a house where we could stay. The next morning she went up the mountain, very near the town at first, going up a little higher each morning until she found a small abandoned house. "This will do," she decided.

We started packing a very few of our possessions: a change of clothes and some necessities. "Just a very few things," Father told us, "just a few pieces that you can carry in one hand."

On the night agreed upon by the four families, we had supper and waited until it was time to leave. We could hardly contain ourselves; I could not put a name to how I felt, shivering in this warm night, bursting with excitement, and most certainly, with anticipation, too. But not fear. I cannot recall ever being afraid when my father was near. Around midnight, Father was ready.

"Time to go," he told us quietly. We picked up our bundles and just walked out of town, silently, careful not to attract attention to ourselves.

The road to the mountain was just a footpath and we went single file. The night was vast with a confusion of stars, and as unruly as the way I felt, my heart thumping inside my chest. The stars were not enough to light our way and I held on to Father's hand as we followed our path cautiously in the dark, careful not to stray from the trail.

Along the way we passed huts built far from the road, lonely silhouettes against the faint light of stars.

We arrived at our destination about mid-morning. The house was just a hut made of bamboo and *nipa*. There was only one room, no piece of furniture or anything, just an empty room. A small shed on bare ground extended from the entrance. This became muddy on rainy days but it served us well as a kitchen. There was a small stream meandering nearby, and we were grateful for that. Here, my sisters washed our pots and pans and did our laundry. It was also a nice stream to take a bath in; the water flowed clear and clean.

We heard later that when the other townspeople woke up the next day and found out that our families were not in our houses anymore, they hurriedly packed their belongings and left town, too.

Mother always had a practical mind. She had packed a few of my sisters' old school uniforms in the bundle she brought with her. Clothes were always welcome tender. She bartered these uniforms for rice, bananas, *camote* and even an occasional chicken, eggs and fish.

We stayed there about a month and a half.

-    -   -   -

News came to us that a US gunboat was approaching Malitbog. I do not know who brought us the news, but Father did not even consider its implications, or the danger we might be running into.

"Time to go down," he told us, "hurry, hurry." We were all very excited, immediately rushing down the mountain path. Mother was not sure if this was the safe thing to do, but Father was resolute, and we all followed him. Along the way we met Emit and some guerrillas.

"What's happening now, Emit?" Father asked.

"They're here, *Tio* Dioni, they're here." Emit was triumphant. "The Americans are here, *Tia* Merced."

We started laughing and hugging each other, with relief, joy, and exhilaration. "Thank God, thank God."

"Come now, let's go," said Emit, his voice ringing in the morning sun.

We all hurried along excitedly, running down the mountain as though we were going to a fiesta. Then we heard cannon bursts. We ran to the top of a promontory. I could see it still, the sight that greeted us on that bluff: at our feet, the whole town spread out before us, the silver sea sparkling under the sun, the gunboat on the water, the smoke rising from the town each time a cannonball hit a target.

"It's all right now," Emit reassured us. "There's no danger. Those navy men know what they're doing. They're shelling the *Casa* in case there are still Japanese left there. The town is safe. Let's go."

We did not linger. We went directly to our house. My mother and sisters wanted to make sure we would be there before any of the other townspeople came down and maybe started looting the house.

We found our things scattered all over the place, pictures stripped from walls, our books strewn all over the floor. The looting had already been done. Apparently, the Japanese contingent that had been left behind had gone over the house, emptying drawers and closets where we stored our clothes. Before we left for the mountains, my sisters had buried chinaware and our other valuables in the air raid shelter downstairs. They ran down to check if the items were still there.

"Thank God," they exclaimed, relieved. Everything was intact!

-    -   -   -

The Americans had shelled enemy stronghold, stormed the island. They overran the town but by the time they shelled the *Casa*, the Japanese had already flown.

We ran to the shore, breaking through the crowds as American landing barges swept toward land. The front of one landing barge flapped open, a jeep rolled out, and American soldiers poured out onto the beach. People had lined the streets, laughing, waving, shouting welcome. The Americans were as exhilarated as we were. They were laughing and waving, too. An American driving a jeep scooped me up and carried me aloft to his jeep. Perhaps I was the first boy he had seen in a long time who had yellow hair, hair bleached yellow from too much sun. And so it started. The liberation that had been so awaited for, so longed for, liberation from the oppressors, liberation from freedoms curtailed, and most of all, in my little boy's requirements, liberation from hunger.

They were in our house everyday, relieved to find people with whom they could carry on a conversation in fluent English and Spanish. And carry on they did, about their families, about the horrors they just went through, about the exhilarating prospect of going back home.

One of them, very excited, told my sisters, "My mom bought a *maquina.*"

"A *maquina*?" My sisters were puzzled.

"Yes, a Ford."

"Oh, a Ford!" exclaimed my sisters laughing, as understanding dawned. A *maquina* in these parts meant a sewing machine. A Ford was definitely something else.

In exchange they brought food---fat chunks of chocolates, *Whitman's* and *Almond Roca,* the boxes proclaimed, large tins of butter and cheese and ham, extremely large cans of corned beef hash that people refused to eat, *hash* sounding suspiciously like the local word for snake. They threw out the contents, and used the cans to carry water in, until they were told that *hash* was not the sinister thing they thought at first.

The Americans also brought huge cans of corned beef. Ramon, just starving for meat, opened one as big as a loaf of bread. He heated it up, and sat down to enjoy the entire platter all by himself. He threw up afterwards. That was it for corned beef! He did not touch the stuff again.

After a long, dry spell, with nothing to fill our stomach but rice porridge, this was more indulgence than we could ask for, this luxury of ham and cheese and coffee, and Whitman's chocolates for dessert. They also brought us cartons of food, K-rations they called them, packaged breakfasts and lunches and dinners, always with a small packet of cigarettes inside.

I brought some boxes with me down to the riverbank, and under the shade of the solitary tree, I gorged myself. After the K-ration and Whitman's chocolates, full and satiated, I reclined on the grass and smoked the cigarettes from the K-ration. It was a waste to throw them away. Waste not, want not, weren't we often told? I sputtered and coughed a few times as the smoke invaded my nostrils and my breathing passages; but that did not take too long and I did not mind it one bit at all.

There I lay, drinking in the golden day, drunk with happiness, a huge smile crowding my face, while tattered clouds above scattered across the blinding blue sky, the river at my feet shimmered and idled to the sea, and the sun strengthened through the leaves and cast dappled shadows on my body.

-   -   -   -

And so we reconstructed our lives. First we searched for family members who had disappeared.

When the family exhausted all means of finding Lolita and hope that she was alive became dimmer each day, there was the crushing task of looking for her body. They dug up the back of the *Casa*, but they never found her. The family carried out the same daunting task of finding Ed and Lito Coromina but came up against the same sad, blank wall.

Then we heard stories that shed light on what happened to Ed and Lito.

With the Americans winning the war and the Pacific war coming to an end and their defeat imminent, the Japanese made preparations to leave town.

Ed could have saved himself, a local man told us. He was imprisoned in the *Casa* with Ed, he said. "I have this friend with the VC," the Volunteer Constabulary, he continued his story, "he heard the Japanese saying that they were going to take all the prisoners with them on the boat when they leave town, to where he did not know, but he told me that if we could, we had better make our escape as soon as possible. I repeated this story to Ed and told him that I was going to escape immediately. I told him to come with me as I knew the way better than he did. 'I can't do that,' Ed told me, 'I have a wife and daughter and there's the family to think of. The Japanese will surely take it out on them if I escape.' I told him that his chance for survival was zero once they get him on that boat. He thanked me but said there was nothing he could do. Knowing the Japanese, I knew he was right. The next night I made my escape."

We heard a similar poignant story about Lito.

He was imprisoned in the schoolhouse with one of the local men. This man also heard that the Japanese were going to take all the prisoners in the boat with them when they left town. In an eerie echo of the local man's story about Ed, this man told Lito that he would make his escape and told Lito that he had better come with him. It was not very hard to escape through the back of the schoolhouse, which was dense with vegetation, and the mountains were not very far. He knew the way and he could take Lito with him. But the two brothers were born and brought up in the same honorable tradition, where saving one's own skin without regard for others' was not life's primary consideration.

"I can't do that," Lito echoed Ed's concern. "I have the family to think of. What if my escape angered the Japanese and they took their revenge on the family or on *Tio* Agustin?" That he thought specifically of *Tio* Agustin was easy to understand. *Tio* Agustin was the kindest of men, the uncle everybody loved, the uncle everyone was proud to have, everybody's favorite uncle.

The next day, the man made his escape.

Another prisoner was in the *Casa* with Ed and he, too, told us his story. He was a spear-fisher, one of the many fishermen in our town who earned their living fishing underwater. He was with Ed during the last days of the war, he told us.

"When the Japanese learned that the Americans were landing in Leyte and were expected to reach our town soon," he told us, "they prepared their retreat. They tied up all of us prisoners, herded us into their boat, then they tied huge rocks on us to weigh us down." When they reached the deep part of the bay, the Japanese pitched all the rope-tied men overboard, then made their getaway. This man, who grew up swimming these waters, was able to hold his breath long enough to free himself from the rocks and the ropes that bound him. He believed that Ed was one of those prisoners, too. But Ed, born and bred in the city, whose encounters with seawater were for pure pleasure, could not have stood a chance. If he was there.

The loss of these two brothers brought him pain, but *Tio* Agustin was surely very proud of them, as we were, as we all were.

At least so much we heard about Ed. With Lito we could only conjecture. Maybe they met the same fate. Maybe. Not that the knowledge would have lessened the grief. With Ed and another brother, Alfonso, Lito was one of three sons the Corominas lost in the war. He was all of nineteen!

24

The war was over in our part of the world. It was time to move on.

A few months later, a US gunboat came to Malitbog bringing Don Andres Soriano of the San Miguel Corporation that produced the renowned beer. He was commissioned as a colonel when the war started in the Philippines and he served as an aide to General Douglas MacArthur. With him in the US gunboat were two American businessmen.

Don Andres came down from the gunboat first. He and Father embraced like long-lost friends, smiling broadly, talking as of something they just discussed yesterday. We did not even know that they knew each other. This was how my father was: Like a true Basque, he formed friendships that lasted to the end of his life. There was Buena Cincunegui; their friendship went way back in Basque land. My father and sisters visited his family in Biarritz when they came out from Spain. He was still very much a friend. So was Toñing Cruz, who was a friend since way back when in Spain, whose two daughters, Nena and Nenita, lived in our house during the war, and whose son, Raul, initiated me to the Drinkers' Club. And of course there was *Tio* Lorenzo; he and Father were still in their teens when they first went to school together in Guernica, and later in Eton.

"These are my children," Father said, as he presented us to Don Andres.

"Is there anything I can do for you?" Don Andres asked, probably noting how thin we all were. The years of deprivation were long. It would take as long to put flesh on our bones. "Is there anything you want?"

"Bread," Juanita said with alacrity.

"I'm sure that can easily be arranged," Don Andres said.

From within the galleys of the gunboat, Don Andres' men produced loaves of bread thicker than my scrawny arms. We thanked them profusely and hurried home while Father brought Don Andres and the two American businessmen to the villa to confer with *Tio* Lorenzo.

A long time had passed since we last ate fresh bread, much too long, and we had almost forgotten what an extravagance it was to eat hot bread spread thickly with butter that melted in the mouth like silk.

Although the Americans had liberated Leyte, the war was not over in other parts of the country, or in the Pacific.

The United States Army needed abaca to make netting for camouflage, among other things. The Americans were interested in reviving the Philippine abaca business. During all the war years they tried synthetic cord as well as abaca from South America, and found that the Philippine variety of abaca was better and stronger than the synthetic cord that the navy and merchant ships used. The Americans were in a hurry to get back into business with the Philippines to get this much-needed product.

The American businessmen had a proposal: *Tio* Lorenzo and Father would buy the abaca for the Far East Economic Administration of the United States. As an incentive to farmers to plant their lands in abaca again, the FEEA proposed to pay for the hemp in cash and goods. Furthermore, they would provide a six-by-six truck to transport the abaca from Malitbog to Tacloban, the capital of the province.

But *Tio* Lorenzo and Father did not have the capital to start the business. The farmers needed money to start planting, money which neither *Tio* Lorenzo nor Father had.

Tio Lorenzo went to Cebu to tell his brothers and sisters that there was a big opportunity offered by the American Government to restart the abaca business. It augured to be very lucrative because they would be the first in the Philippines to do this, as had been proposed by the American businessmen. However, *Tio* Lorenzo's brothers and sisters were not willing to contribute. They didn't have money to invest, they said. *Tio* Lorenzo came back to Malitbog without a single centavo from his family. It should be noted that *Tio* Lorenzo made this trip to Cebu on a small sailboat good for only two or three people. One can imagine how disappointed he must have been to have made such a hazardous trip for nothing.

Of course everybody in town knew about the American proposal. People were quite excited about it, and very disappointed when they heard that *Tio* Lorenzo's family had not come up with the money.

Molong Oben was one of the farmers in town. When his mother heard that *Tio* Lorenzo came back from Cebu empty-handed, she offered him money that she had saved during the war.

And so *Tio* Lorenzo, together again with Father, started the business with this money from Molong Oben's mother.

It was a good plan. The war had bled the country, and the town, dry. There was no commerce, very little money, and not much that money could buy. But there was plenty of land to plant. The people were hungry for the material goods they could get for their abaca, and the lands that had been laid to waste grew green again.

With the six-by-six truck provided by the Americans, *Tio* Lorenzo and Father traveled the interior towns buying abaca. When the truck was fully loaded, they brought the abaca to Tacloban where a Chinese businessman representing the Americans bought the abaca partly paying in cash and partly in goods. The truck came back packed with textiles, canned goods, cigarettes, men's denim shirts, pants and overalls. Later, the goods included bales of used clothing that were very much needed and appreciated by the abaca producers. Father's share of the business was also partly in cash and partly in goods, the larger part of which was the bales of used clothing, which Mother sold in the outlying towns whenever there was a market day.

The town sprang back to life and commerce that had become moribund during the war hummed with activity again.

Raul Cruz was still in town, the same Raul Cruz who had introduced me to the pleasures of the bottle, or the lack of them, as

there certainly was no pleasure having my butt whacked by my
mother. Now he was one of my father's drivers.

He asked us if we wanted to go with him and another friend,
Pete Jarque, to Tanawan, a town near Tacloban. There was going
to be a USO show for GIs by American entertainers, he told us.
Sure, we said, if he would ask Father's permission. Father said yes,
but make sure he brought us home on time; it wasn't good for
children to be out late. So to Tanawan we went: Raul, Pete Jarque,
my brother, and I.

The airfield was filled with noisy GIs who showed their
appreciation with hoots and shouts and laughter and applause. It
was a very good show. The man who played the trumpet so
marvelously, Raul told us, was called Harry James, and the
gorgeous blonde who danced and sang on the stage was his wife,
Betty Grable. That's why he did not mind her cavorting there in
front of an airfield of hooting men: her short skirt showed a lot of
her splendid legs.

The show ended at 2 in the morning, well past the curfew
imposed on us, and Father gave Raul a scolding when he brought
us back. But it was a great show, and started me on the road to the
joys of Harry James and Betty Grable, Broadway and Hollywood
musicals, and a lifelong love of music and dance.

- -   -   -

American stock-of-war material that was no longer needed in
peacetime was staggering, and so was the waste. All the traveling
that we did took its toll on our truck. We arrived in Tacloban one
early morning with our truck limping. Father and the mechanic
came down from the truck to see what was wrong.

"I guess we lost some nuts and bolts along the way," the
mechanic said. "We will have to take it in for repairs." We
proceeded to the American repair shop. Father asked the GI
minding the shop if we could have the truck repaired there.

The GI looked at us, then at the truck, without interest. "Oh,
why bother? Too much trouble," he answered, dismissing us.
"There, take another one."

"Another what?" Father asked, astonished.

The GI looked at Father and explained, as to a child. "You leave your truck over there," he pointed to one direction, "and you pick up another truck from over there," he pointed to another direction, a huge enclosure filled with trucks. We went over to this yard, once in a while darting a startled glance at each other and at the GI, who had already forgotten us. Father and our mechanic checked a few trucks and picked one they decided was better than ours. We came home with a new old truck, at least newer than the truck we brought out.

We had heard these stories before. The Americans would fill an MLC, a mechanized landing craft, with equipment that they found too bothersome to repair, then dump it into the sea. Trucks, tanks, jeeps, everything that fell into the category of *why bother, too much trouble* shared the same fate. Maybe that was where our truck, limping but far from dead, found itself, prematurely laid out in its final resting place at the bottom of the sea.

Everybody who could and would, wheeled and dealt.

From Tacloban to about sixty kilometers south, Americans had planted gasoline pumping stations, unattended, unlocked sheds with pumps and nozzles where any vehicle with military markings could withdraw gas. Maybe they trusted the civilians too much, maybe there were not enough civilian vehicles roaming the countryside for them to worry about, maybe there was just too much inventory for them to monitor.

I heard stories from other drivers that sometimes when Father did not go with the truck to Tacloban, one driver would load the truck with an empty barrel or two. After delivering the abaca, he would sneak out, fill the drums with gasoline from the orphaned pumps, sell them to other points south where there were no pumping stations, and earn a few fast bucks, his sweat and adrenaline his only investment, knowing that if Father found out, he could kiss his job goodbye.

But Filipinos did not corner the market on the fast, dishonest buck. Many GIs made a fortune from all this waste. Trucks and other war material littered the countryside. Ong, one of Father's traders, told of ordering goods from an American Army personnel who came soliciting. A hundred bags of flour, Ong ordered, a hundred cartons of canned fruits, a hundred of this, a hundred of that. It seemed the lowly dozen was not mentioned anymore. In the evening, Ong related, the American came with an army truck and discharged Ong's order into his warehouse.

"You can keep the truck," the American told him. "I'm not taking it back."

"Oh, no, no, no," Ong protested, quite scared. An army truck on his property would broadcast the transaction, done all the time but still not legal. He ran briskly after the departing American. "I don't need the truck. You can have it, there, take it, take it. Please. Thank you. Thank you."

25

The war had ended!

Hitler had killed himself, Nazi Germany was defeated, Japan finally surrendered. General Douglas MacArthur, Supreme Commander for the Allied Powers, landed in Japan in his C-54 aircraft named "Bataan" to start the process of rebuilding postwar Japan.

Opportunities for business sprouted all over the place and *Tio* Lorenzo wanted to seize these opportunities, enter this lucrative market that the overflowing American surplus created. He told Father of barges that the Americans were disposing of, landing barges that could bring him and Father to the neighboring islands to buy abaca in half the time it would take them if they went by truck. These did not cost a lot; *Tio* Lorenzo told Father he was buying one, and would Father want one for himself, too?

Father had been aching to go back to work, and knew that he would have a good start with a barge. He could pay for the barge with money Mother saved from the sale of the goods he received as part of his share of the arrangement with the Far East Economic Administration of the United States. Accompanied by my brother Ramon, our mechanic, and our driver, Father went to Tacloban and came back with two barges.

The barges were old things, survivors of war, but they would do quite well, Father said. Although the exteriors were encrusted with barnacles and needed a lot of cleaning up, the internal mechanisms could still work for a good many years. Father moored our barge near the wharf. He, my brother, our mechanic, and I set out to work on it. We scraped away the rust, the barnacles and other things that had attached themselves to its sides.

One such day, Jacinto Aberásturi, my father's nephew, came to the wharf where we were working. "What are you doing with our barge?" Jacinto asked. Father looked up from where he was busily prying the barnacles from the side of the barge. He looked very puzzled.

"Your barge? What do you mean *your* barge?" asked Father.

"Well, isn't this *Hijos*' barge?" said Jacinto.

"*Hijos*' barge?" Father looked at Jacinto, hardly believing what he heard. "What *Hijos* are you talking about?" *Hijos* had been moribund all through the war. "I paid for this with my own money."

"*Ladron*." Thief. Jacinto spat out. "Paid for it with what?"

Ladron. The word, flung at him by his nephew, was like a shot that tore straight through his heart and left him too stunned for words. His brows gathered inward, his face darkened, his eyes blazed at Jacinto. But he never had to explain himself to anybody, much less to this son of his own brother, who, after all these years, should have known better than to cast aspersion on his integrity. Father reined himself in.

"Why don't you just go ask Lorenzo?" he said, shaking his head, throwing down the scraper he was holding, disgust written on his face. Disgust, not humiliation.

"Well, if it is yours, what is it doing by our wharf?" said Jacinto.

"Your wharf?" This was the wharf of *Hijos de* F. Escaño. Father left Spain at the urging of *Tio* Lorenzo, to help him put to right the affairs of this compan*y, w*hich at that time was in complete disarray and on the brink of bankruptcy. This Father did, worked with *Tio* Lorenzo for some thirty years. All these years, before the war broke out, and *Hijos* was still in lucrative operation, *Tio* Lorenzo was the president of *Hijos*, and Father was manager. Even though *Hijos*, and indeed all other businesses in the country, stood still during the war and had not resumed operations at this time, Father just presumed that he still had the right to use *Hijos*' wharf. But he was not going to argue this point.

"Very well, then," said Father, "it will do somewhere else." Without further fuss, we moved the barge to the land across the river at the back of our house. Then we could just push it out into the sea when we needed to use it, Father said.

-   -   -   -

Even before this incident, Father had already heard rumblings of complaints from members of Jacinto's family that Father was filling a role in the company that Jacinto could fill himself. After all, Father was not really an Escaño. His brother just happened to be married to the oldest Escaño daughter, Justina. Although Father was married to the first cousin of *Tio* Lorenzo, my mother was only a niece of the matriarch of the family. Father recognized that Jacinto Aberásturi, whose mother, Justina, was an Escaño, had more right to manage *Hijos de* F. Escaño, if he so desired. Father never intruded where he was not wanted, much less be in a situation where a shadow was cast on his integrity. Without much deliberation on his part, he told *Tio* Lorenzo it was time he went on his own.

Tio Lorenzo protested vigorously. "There may not be much going on with *Hijos* now," *Tio* Lorenzo said, "But there should be in a little while. Just stick it out a little bit." If anyone knew my father to the core, it was *Tio* Lorenzo. In all the years they had known each other, Father had never given *Tio* Lorenzo reason to doubt him; there had never been a single ambiguous incident. But Father was adamant. "It's all right," he told *Tio* Lorenzo. "There's enough merchandise to go around. I'll manage."

-   -   -   -

Through all the years of buying abaca, Father had developed a network of abaca suppliers, Chinese traders with whom he had developed an excellent business relationship. When one of them, Ping Guan, heard that Father was now on his own, he approached Father and offered him a partnership.

"I have the money," Ping-Guan said, "but I do not have somebody with whom I could trust to be my partner." So Father set out on a new venture in which he was part owner, contributing to the enterprise his own barge, his capacity for hard work, and an uprightness that was never questioned in our town or in the entire province. With Ping-Guan as partner, Father traveled the area, making trips to Cebu and the Visayan region, buying abaca. He rose before dawn, not resting until long after dusk.

If he was outraged by Jacinto's insinuation that he had expropriated what was not his, he did not show it. He did not feel obliged to answer to anybody. Jacinto might have accused him of not having had enough money to buy the barge on his own and of therefore raiding *Hijos'* coffers, if in fact there was still anything left there to raid after the war, but Father knew nobody would believe that. In all the years he had been with *Hijos*, in all the years he lived in this town, there had not been a single occasion when his integrity was placed in doubt. He lived his life on principles that he never compromised, on an honesty that his business associates had come to trust, on values that everyone in our town had come to identify with him. And, except when he brought them up to teach lessons to his children, he never felt the need to explain.

Did it hurt him more that these accusations came, not from one of Mother's cousins, but from the son of his own brother, his own blood? It must have cut deeply, but he never let on. He simply withdrew from the situation. The matter was never mentioned again in our presence, at least not in mine, but sometimes, I would catch a look on his face when Jacinto's name was mentioned, a quick withdrawal from the conversation, a closing of his face as though some inner shutters had been drawn. That look stirred up longings in me to assure him that he need not worry about how I felt. But we shared with our parents this bent for keeping passions private, feelings unspoken, emotions out of sight. He must have known that this accusation to his face in front of his sons did not reduce him in our sight. The examples he had set throughout our lives spoke for him.

-    -   -   -

Some time before this, a man from a town across the bay who had done some jobs for Father borrowed a thousand pesos from him, and signed out a ten-hectare piece of his land to Father as collateral. In those days, land could be had for a pittance, and a thousand was quite a lot of money. My parents promptly forgot about the loan until years later when they received a notice from the Court informing them that the fellow had died and we were now in possession of a substantial rice land. Father asked us how we felt about the court order.

"But of course we take possession," said Ramon, without batting an eyelash, much less having second thoughts about taking ownership of something we did not ask for but was dropped on our laps by the court of the land. "It's legally ours now. The court said so."

"Legally, yes," said Father, "but morally?"

Knowing Father, with his steadfast moral convictions, we knew where this conversation was going. "Are you saying we're not taking it?"

To give an idea of how bountiful a ten-hectare rice land was, a hectare produced, twice a year, about eighty sacks of unmilled rice, a hundred when the harvest was good. Eighty sacks of unmilled rice would produce forty sacks when milled. Understandably, my brother, and of course, I, too, were reluctant, to say the least, to hand over this until-now-forgotten and quite-unexpected, granary.

"He had children," said Father. "That land belongs to them."

"Even though the Court rules otherwise?" Even though.

This was how life was lived in our house. What was legal was not necessarily moral. Some things the law permitted, the conscience would not allow. Father had always been a very compassionate man. That man had borrowed money because he needed it; Father could not in all conscience take advantage of that need. Also, as he said, the fellow had children, obviously in need, too, or they could have tried to raise the money and reclaim their land.

Father sent one of our workers across the bay, to the surely very surprised children of that man, to tell them to just pay back the thousand their father owed us, no interest was mentioned, and they could have their land back. Our worker came back with the money, Father paid for our man's expenses, and for the thousand that was borrowed, Father got back less than eight hundred.

No, we did not get the rice land. But we were never more proud.

- -   -   -

My father's was a landed family. When his siblings, *Tia* Margarita, *Tia* Josefa, and *Tio* Raimundo died, they left their entire estate in Spain to Father. Their oldest brother, Bruno, had already taken out his own share a long time before. After Father died, a Capuchin priest traveled all the way from Spain to Malitbog to ask us to sell to their order a portion of our land planted in pine trees that stood outside their monastery. They were getting crowded and wanted to expand. They had already made overtures through our cousins in Spain who took care of our lands, but we had resisted. We knew Father wanted us to hold on to our lands in Spain. If the Capuchin priest had just written, we surely would have declined. We did not want to chop off parts of our inheritance to sell, noble though the request was. But he was already in our house, arranging himself comfortably into furniture too cramped for his hefty size, and looked as though he would stay until he got what he came for. Reluctantly, we acquiesced. After the sale, Cristina and Juanita gave a share of the proceeds to the heirs of my father's brother, Bruno Aberásturi. "If that property was left to them," I asked Juanita, "do you think we would see a cent from it?"

But I knew what her answer would be. "It's all right," she said, "we live our lives as we believe is right, we don't answer for others and how they live theirs." Spoken like a true daughter of her father.

Father started molding his children's character early on.

One afternoon Emiliana came home from school early. "You're home?" my father asked, concerned. "Are you all right?"

"Oh, I'm all right," she replied. "Teacher sent me home. The other girls are cleaning the bathrooms. Teacher said I don't have to do it."

"And why not?" My father's voice changed from concern to anticipated displeasure. All his attention was now turned on her.

"She said I'm an Aberásturi and I don't have to clean bathrooms."

"Is that so!" said my father, stressing each word. "Well, you tell your teacher that you are not to be given special treatment. Listen to me," he said in a very stern voice, looking at Emiliana with a very stern face, "you do what you are supposed to do. Don't expect other people to do your work for you. And don't expect special treatment. Now, you go back there and clean those bathrooms just like the rest of the girls."

- - - -

Jacinto had a son, Vicente. He spent his days sitting by the window, watching people pass by. He would call out to them and engage them in trivial conversation. After the "*Ladron*" incident, he would watch for Father as he walked past their house on his way to work.

"Oh, Moustache, oh, Moustache," he would call out, impertinently referring to Father's singularly bushy one, "where did you get the money to buy the barge?" These taunts, coming from a grown man with children, who spent his days sitting by the window instead of going out to work to provide for them, were more pathetic than infuriating, and Father did not pay them heed.

Only once did he get a rise from Father. "Why don't you come down here, then I will tell you where that money came from," said Father, standing on the street, looking up at him. After a long time of getting nowhere with Father, this reaction, though calm, unnerved Jacinto. "Oh, you threatened me, you threatened me. I'll go to the police, I'll go to the police."

"Oh, you go to hell, you crazy coot," said Father and went on his way.

Vicente sat in stunned silence for a while, collecting his wits. With Father safely gone, he came out of their house and went to the police station, a few meters away from their house, to make a report. He made the policemen's day, gave them a merry respite from the humdrum chore of policing a town where most of the melodrama was provided by the family, anyway.

"From what we see and hear every morning," the policeman on duty told him, "it should be *Señor* Dioni who should be filing a report of harassment against you."

26

With the war now over, *Hijos* gathered up its resources, poised to resume business again. *Tio* Lorenzo's brothers and sisters summoned him to Cebu. They wanted him to reorganize and start the company again. When he came back from Cebu, Juanita had a talk with *Tia* Piling.

"Is he going to reorganize *Hijos*?" Juanita asked.

"He said he would, on one condition," said *Tia* Piling, "that Dioni will still be manager, as he was before the war. But Teresa objected to it." Teresa was another sister of *Tio* Lorenzo and held the majority stocks of *Hijos*. She had been buying stocks from other stockholders who, after many years of holding on to stocks that did not bear any dividends, were willing to sell.

But *Tio* Lorenzo stood firm---he would come only if Father managed *Hijos* again.

In an effort to sever *Tio* Lorenzo's ties with my father, ties that had stayed fast for some thirty years, Jose Mari Aberásturi Gonzalez, son of our cousin Emiling Aberásturi Gonzalez, approached Juanita. "Why doesn't *Tio* Dioni manage one of Cesar's *hacienda*s?" Jose Mari proposed to my sister. "So much land. *Tio* Dioni would be an asset to Cesar and Cristina." That was a good plan, if Father would take leave of his senses, give up a business he had toiled hard to make into a running success, cross the seas to manage the Lopezes' rice lands and coconut lands, and especially sugarcane lands, an endeavor he knew nothing about.

When he was still the manager of *Hijos*, Father, as did *Tio* Agustin and *Tio* Lorenzo, drew from their salary just enough for what they needed, leaving the rest for the company to use if it needed to. These salaries and withdrawals were entered in the books of the company by Juan Cañon, the *tenidor de libros*, the keeper of the books of *Hijos*.

Tio Agustin financed his lifestyle this way, taking out only what he needed, leaving the rest in the company coffers. But his lifestyle differed from the others' and he ended up taking out more than he put in. After the war, *Hijos* decided to clean up the books.

Tio Agustin took walks most afternoons, from his villa on one side of town, past our house on the other end. When he did, he would drop by and spend a few minutes talking to my parents. One day he told them he had signed away all his *Hijos* shares to pay for what he owed the company. Jose Mari Gonzalez had come and stayed at *Tio* Agustin's villa, as he and his parents and sisters always did when they came to town to visit, eschewing the *Casa* where a crowd always stayed. He left with papers bearing *Tio* Agustin's signature, signing away all *Tio* Agustin's shares in the company. He had owed *Hijos*, *Tio* Agustin told my parents. *Hijos* wanted his shares as payment. No, he said when my parents asked, *Hijos* did not want payment installment-style, and he did not have the ready resources to pay full-this-instant style.

Financially, signing away his shares was not much of a disaster for *Tio* Agustin. He owned lands that brought him more wealth than he needed. But being cut off from the company that bore his name, that he had helped build, broke his heart.

In matters like these, talks always followed. Everyone said it was just Emit. The thought of Emit inheriting *Tio* Agustin's shares, and having his foot, and everything that came with it, inside *Hijos'* door, was just too disturbing a prospect to contemplate, too alarming that it outweighed the ultimate issue of stripping *Tio* Agustin of his shares.

-     -   -   -

Father had done the same thing, leaving a large part of his salary with *Hijos*, taking out only a small part for our immediate needs. Our needs were few, our wants fewer. I do not remember my parents indulging in any luxury. They saved and saved, even as our lands flowed with grains and produced bounteous fruits, and our fortunes much improved.

When *Tio* Lorenzo heard of a vast tract of land in Mindanao that the owners wanted to sell, he, *Tio* Pepe Coromina (the husband of *Tio* Lorenzo's sister Paz), and Father put up money to buy the property. Father went into a new partnership, a truly large acquisition that was planted extensively in rice and coconut.

In his travels to the north to buy abaca, Father's Chinese traders told of a large tract of coconut and rice land that had been put up for sale, not as large as the Mindanao property, but still large enough. He bought this, too. As their landholdings expanded, so did the money my parents put aside. Their savings multiplied while our warehouse overflowed.

Later, *Tio* Pepe Coromina sold his share of the land to *Tio* Lorenzo and Father. As much as Father believed in using his money to acquire land, *Tio* Lorenzo believed that his money would do better invested in business. When he decided to sell the Mindanao property, he asked Father if he would like to buy him out. Thus Father became sole owner of this huge property, too.

-    -   -   -

After Father died, my sisters found among his papers a signed statement by Juan Cañon, the bookkeeper of *Hijos*, of what he had earned while at *Hijos*, which far exceeded what he withdrew, which meant that he still had money coming to him. My sisters went to *Hijos* in Cebu to get the remainder of Father's salary. They were told that these were new times, the company had started anew and the company books were also new, and why did they not come forward with this information after the war ended?

"We did not know about this until after he died and we looked through his papers. Besides, it is still the same company, owned by the same people." Operated on the same principles, or so they hoped.

"Well, you should have come forward, then."

"Does this mean that his money just got swallowed up?"

It did. My sisters came back empty-handed.

27

When his siblings told *Tio* Lorenzo that *Hijos* could not absorb Father as manager, *Tio* Lorenzo declined their offer to resurrect *Hijos*. He then decided to put up his own company. He went back to Father and together they pooled their resources. Father went to Ping Guan and they arranged to dissolve their partnership. He sold the barge, sold shares from his other holdings, took out money from savings. With a 60/40 division of ownership, he and *Tio* Lorenzo established a new company and called it *L. Escaño & Company*. Then Father and *Tio* Lorenzo went back to working together again, in a partnership so like a marriage, which lasted a lifetime, until death did them part.

Tio Lorenzo's siblings who composed *Hijos* were not pleased that *Tio* Lorenzo used *L. Escaño* to name his new company. People might confuse the two, they objected. "What name am I supposed to use," *Tio* Lorenzo said, "since that happens to be my name?" What indeed?

Father, my brother and Otic Escaño went to Tacloban to buy surplus US Navy minesweepers, which they converted to passenger ships. *Tio* Lorenzo then bought a property on the other side of town, converted it into an abaca press and a warehouse, and built a wharf near it. Molong Oben, whose mother lent *Tio* Lorenzo the money to start the business with the Far East Economic Administration, established a labor union. *Tio* Lorenzo used Molong Oben's laborers to work for *L. Escaño* at the abaca press and later at the pier to load the abaca, and other cargo, unto the ships.

Father went on with his usual way of life. He rose at 5 in the morning, listened to his radio while he had his coffee, walked to work, and was at his office before seven.

With the tireless dedication they expended on the business, Tio Lorenzo's unerring business acumen, and Father's impeccable business relationship with the abaca traders, *L. Escaño* quickly prospered. Before long, they had acquired several six-by-six trucks and then five ships, the *Seamaster, Pilarica, Lourdes, Milagrosa,* and *Bonlico,* which plied the Visayas-Mindanao waters.

Father traveled the Pacific coastal towns buying abaca. He would buy some hundred tons a week, sometimes a hundred fifty, entirely filling the bowels of the ships, cleaning up the available abaca as far away south as Cagayan de Oro and Mangagoy, and the pacific towns west of Mindanao.

-      -   -   -

Tio Lorenzo was the exemplar of timesaving engineering. Passengers trusted the ships' schedules. When a ship was scheduled to leave at 8, it left at 8. Pulling out of the harbor at half past was already considered late, and the *Jefe de Viaje,* the ship's purser, had some answering to do or risked being fired, which happened often. But though impatient to a fault, *Tio* Lorenzo also had a good heart. The person fired just came back to work the next day, the firing was not mentioned, and business proceeded as usual.

Others learned their lessons well. When *Tio* Lorenzo and *Tia* Piling went to Cebu, which was often, *Tio* Lorenzo was on board fifteen minutes before departure time; *Tia* Piling followed a few minutes later. Once, when after the designated time the ship was still moored, *Tio* Lorenzo inquired, "Why aren't we pulling up anchors?"

"*Señor,*" the ship captain said, "*Señora Piling* is not on board yet."

"Well, then," said *Tio* Lorenzo, "the ship leaves without her."

It did.

Tia Piling arrived a few minutes later, at the wharf empty of husband and ship.

-      -   -   -

Tio Lorenzo kept a tight rein on the operations of the shipping side of the business while Father took charge of the abaca side. However, some matters were too delicate for the ships' captains to bring to *Tio* Lorenzo's attention and they sought refuge in Father's. One ship captain reported complaints from ship employees that they were being fed rice and dried fish all the time. Since *Tio* Lorenzo's son, Roque, was the officer charged with purchasing the ships' provisions, which definitely included meals for ship workers more substantial than dried fish and rice, Father conferred with *Tio* Lorenzo. It seemed that there were other complaints as well from female passengers about unwelcome advances from Roque. A formal complaint had actually been filed by one of these lady passengers, which Otic Escaño managed to hush up with hush money, but now women avoided the *L. Escaño* ships, lest they found themselves the object of Roque's unwanted attentions. *Tio* Lorenzo said that Father should do what he had to do, as he was the one to whom the report was given, and he, *Tio* Lorenzo, would not interfere. In the course of Father's inquiries, he ascertained that the reports were indeed true. He forthwith fired Roque.

Now Roque was at the pier when an *L. Escaño* ship steamed into port; now he was holding a bullhorn, putting down his own father's ships. "Passengers," he boomed, "don't take the *Pilarica*. The *L. Escaño* ships are no-good ships. Take the *Hijos* ships instead. You get a free bottle of Coca-Cola."

These stories would be funny if they weren't pathetic. We cousins chose amusement. Father and *Tio* Lorenzo chose the higher ground.

"Lorenzo, you have got to see this," Father called *Tio* Lorenzo.

As the two men arrived at the pier and watched Roque holding forth, talking passengers out of taking his own father's ships, enticing them with soft-drink promises to take the *Hijos* ships instead, the two started laughing.

"*Ay, que tonto,*" said *Tio* Lorenzo.

-    -   -   -

Roque was not the only peculiar member of our family. We had other strange characters coloring our family picture. Take our cousin Berting, for instance.

Berting was a hypochondriac who dreamed up diseases he was sure he had. His parents spent a lot of money on doctors to convince him that nothing was wrong with him, but not one was able to convince him otherwise.

"My advice to you," said one of his doctors, "is to go down every morning to the beach at the back of your house, plunge into the seawater, take a long swim." Advice, of course, that he ignored.

Later, when his doctors made it known that they were not treating him anymore, which was rather decent of them, considering the resulting financial loss to them, Berting put down a good part of his inheritance on medical paraphernalia so he could cure himself of whatever he was sure ailed him.

He did not choose the really serious diseases, though, nothing that needed an operation, or a transplant. No big C for him, just the middle-of-the-road stuff, grave enough to keep him housebound and not working but not life-threatening enough to keep him to his bed.

His wife was servant, nurse and martyr. He would ask for water. "Just half a glass, I'm not that thirsty, really." She would bring half a glass as told. "I guess I am more thirsty than I thought," he'd say, "bring me more." Back to the kitchen the wife would trudge. This tragicomedy would go on until, tired out from traversing the bedroom to the kitchen and back, which in their huge house was quite a trek, she returned, bearing a pitcher of water.

"Ah, surely you exaggerate," he chided, eyeing the pitcher. "Here," he pushed his glass at her crossly, "just pour a little bit, oops, oops, not too much." He gulped down the little-bit, then extended his glass for more. "Just a little bit more, oops, oops, not too much, I said."

Sick with all the ailments he had chosen for himself, his sex life took strange ups and downs as well. He had sporadic erections that reared their heads, so to speak, at the most inconvenient hours. He would have one in the middle of the afternoon, for instance, when his wife was in the kitchen, and he would summon her with great urgency. "Come now, come now, hurry, before it's gone."

But she had to wash her hands first, or send the children out to the yard on some pretext, or see that the house did not burn down while she was servicing him, so that very often, by the time she reached him, his excitement had quieted down. "There," he would scold her, "it's gone, you took too long."

On those times when she did come on time, however, he must have been potent enough: she bore him nine children.

He was the drugstore's best customer, practically siphoning off the supply of drugs he thought he needed. The drugstore could not order the drug Ativan fast enough. Children can be cruel. When cousins would see one of his children going to the drugstore, they would tease: "What, Ativan again?" or "Oh, oh, we'd better get our Ativan now, before Bert finishes up the drugstore's supply," pretending to rush to the counter ahead of Bert, Berting's son, who would saunter in stony-faced, deaf to their taunts.

Berting did die, very much later, after he had squandered his inheritance on nourishing and pampering and feeding his imagined afflictions. The feeding and nourishing of his children came from other quarters, and there certainly was no pampering there. He left his widow and children destitute and it fell upon the other members of the family to soften their hard times.

Round parents produce square children, we are often told. Berting produced quiet, responsible offspring, who were called 'good children,' who waited at his beck and call, who took turns missing school so that one of them was always there when he beckoned and called; silent, tentative, wing-clipped children, who did not speak unless spoken to, who melted into the background of the family picture, who retreated from the pattern of family life. Later, when his sons were ready for college, we uncles pooled together resources to pay for tuition fees.

-    -   -   -

While *Tio* Lorenzo kept the shipping part of the business thriving strong, the abaca side of the business flourished, too.

Farmers with abaca came to our house at any time of day and they, sweating, fanning themselves with the hem of their shirts, slumping tiredly on the huge protruding roots of the old trees that faced the *bodega*, huffing from the heavy cargo they had slung over their shoulders or borne on their heads from faraway barrios whence they came, always, always, took preference over whatever Father was doing at the time. Most times they came when we were having lunch and Father would leave the table at once to take care of them. Ramon and I would get up, too, and follow him. It was just something we knew we had to do without being told. If we had gone on with lunch, would he have told us to come and help him? I never knew. The thought that we would keep on eating while Father was down there taking care of business was a disgraceful notion that never entered our minds.

These disruptions were a fact of life for us and we never minded them. Many times they were diversions, too, watching Father doing business buying abaca. His skills in numbers were just remarkable, far exceeding mere sums. "Fifty-two kilos," he would say to the seller, weighing the bale, "at sixty-five centavos a kilo," depending on the class of the fiber, "that's ah, thirty-three pesos and ah, eighty centavos," he would conclude, taking a look upward, then a couple of blinks, paper and pen not necessary. The sellers never corrected him, their trust in him explicit. Besides which, of course, they already knew how much their bales were worth, which always matched the figures on the receipts they got for the sale.

Sometimes, Father let us grade and price the abaca ourselves and after a while, we had become abaca experts; we could tell the grade of the abaca by just looking at it. I also took a certain amount of pride showing off my math skills to Father. I would imitate him by doing numbers in my head, happy when I got the numbers right and got a rewarding smile.

-    -   -   -

We had become abaca experts, or so we thought. But then, expert is far from a carefully defined word, as we found out later.

The American government announced it had granted aid to the Philippine government, assistance that would invigorate the abaca export. The American government said they were sending abaca experts to our province to look at the abaca plantations. When the American experts came, we set out to give them a tour of the abaca plantations.

Abaca plants look remarkably like banana plants, except that the abaca leaves are narrower and sharper than the softer and fuller banana leaves. Along the way, we passed a banana plantation. "Now," said one of the American abaca experts, "now, those are healthy-looking abaca plants there," he declared to our amusement, with a flourish of his hand that swept the entire area that was fully planted in bananas.

28

Over the years, Father had cultivated a friendship with the Chinese traders throughout the island who had the money to buy the abaca from the farmers who planted it, and these Chinese traders, acting as middlemen, supplied the main bulk of the fiber that *L. Escaño* needed.

At times these traders' warehouses spilled over with stock and Father had to send the drivers and their helpers to make extra trips to clear out their warehouses. Sometimes, when more trips were needed, the three of us--Father, my brother and I--had to make the extra trip.

We would leave our house at 3 in the morning and by the time the sun had risen, we had already filled a respectable space of the truck with abaca bales, and almost broken our backs in the process, helping the traders' men haul the bales from their warehouses and piling them unto the truck. At least, Father broke his, who could never just stand still while others worked, and Ramon did too, who could not just stand still while our father worked.

"Just choose the smaller bales," Father would tell me, as he'd wipe the film of sweat that glistened on his forehead with his handkerchief, "we shall take care of the larger ones." And I, needing very little invitation, would. I was thin and often sick, and the dust rising from the abaca fibers as we lashed the bales unto the floor of the truck was murder to my troubled sinuses. My father and my brother had the same big build. Except for that time during the war when Father had a fever, I cannot remember him being sick. He always tried then, as much as he could, to spare me from this arduous work. All this work my brother and I did without recompense. It never occurred to us to think of getting paid. We worked because our father did; the concept of work-for-pay never entered our minds.

Breakfast time would find us with one or another of my father's Chinese suppliers, where we would always be invited to share their meal. Most times, Father would demur. "We still have a lot of places to go, the sun is already hard on our backs, and there's not much time."

"*Señor* Dioni," the Chinese trader would press. "Surely a little time spent with friends is not such a loss. Come eat with us." Father knew he could not always refuse.

My father, my brother, and I would sit down to share a meal with these friends who did not put much stock in social graces and amenities---a table bare with no tablecloth, most times, spoons and forks of varying designs, cups and plates with chips on lips and rims, and flies hovering. But the food was always substantial, and quite good---rice, eggs, slices of fried meat, and dried fish, and of course the ubiquitous rice porridge, if one still cared for that at all. There was always rice porridge in these houses. Every hour of night or day, a kettle of porridge would be simmering over a slow fire. But not for me. I had my share of rice porridge to last me a lifetime.

I never cared what I ate here, tired and hungry as I always was; neither did Father, as we found out from these trips. He never showed that he cared about the food we were served, that he minded the mess, that he saw the difference.

One of these traders, Ching, was a thin man with slits for eyes and a smile that was wider than his eyes, stretching from one ear to the other, brightening up the morning. After breakfast, he would always come with us outside his store to bid us goodbye, still talking to Father as though he did not want the visit to end, laughing his eyes to slits, each of them speaking the Visayan dialect, Father perfect but with a reminiscent inflection, the Chinese in his own curious sing-song. Once, when we were outside, Ching had a coughing spell. He whipped out a handkerchief from his pocket and covered his mouth. He went back inside his store, spat on the floor, squashed his spittle like some white bug with his slippered foot. Then he came back outside to finish his goodbyes. Father's gaze never even flickered.

"But why did he have to go back inside the store to spit on his floor?" I asked Father later. "He could have done it right there on the grass outside."

"Well, they have this belief that if they spit outside, they might spit out their good fortune as well." I found this ludicrously funny and had to laugh and Father said, "Different people have different beliefs. Perhaps we have practices that they find laughable, too, but they are never rude enough to show that they are amused, and neither should you." A lesson well taken.

Father's relationships with these traders were beyond reproach. They held him in high respect and remained his loyal friends to the end of his life.

If Father could stand the difference, so could I, and I always enjoyed those breakfasts. But not Juanita. She came with us once, took one look at the mess, went back out, and never entered the premises again. "*Que asco,*" she told Father. How disgusting. She ate breakfast and lunch of biscuits and other sweets in the truck. Father had to make excuses for her when the traders inquired.

As with other commodities for export, the price of abaca fluctuated according to the price dictated by the world market. This was before the advent of the telephone in our province. When this happened, Father had to notify every one of his suppliers all the way up north, which took an entire day. Sometimes Father allowed us to go with him on these trips and when we did, he would drive our car, which was always a treat.

These were some of the many times spent with Father that I so loved.

We own a long stretch of coconut and rice land up north along the way. They call this town MacArthur now. When the Americans landed in Leyte, and General Douglas MacArthur finally returned to Philippine soil as he had grandly promised, American planes rested wing to wing on this strip of beach many, many kilometers long.

Father took this time to check on our *encargado,* the man who supervised our land. Pedro always insisted that we have lunch with them. His wife would go out briskly and kill a chicken and cook it with some vegetables while Father talked business with Pedro. But Father did not relish eating Pedro's chicken when Pedro's children could have larger portions if we did not share their meal. So Father always apprised Pedro that we were having lunch elsewhere before his wife started rushing about looking for a chicken to behead.

Modern buildings, shopping developments, and housing complexes, all in the name of modernization, had sprouted all over the land. This thrust toward growth had reached the northern part of our island, too, and this monster called progress had gobbled up much of the island's pristine charms. In the process, it had spewed out buildings, testaments to modern times. But the Leyte of my youth, the island that stays in my memory, the narrow province with widespread trees, grassy knolls, rushing streams on one side, and coconut trees, white beaches, and deep, clear waters on the other, still remains unsullied in my mind.

When our father took us with him to his travels up north, we children passed through these idyllic places. When time came to eat, we would choose a hillock under a canopy of trees and have a small picnic. Then we would drink from one of the small waterfalls that abounded in these areas. At first we would just wash our hands and our faces, and then, carried away, we would splash water on each other, which was more of a treat. Most parents would admonish their children not to get themselves wet. Father never did. When he let us loose, he let us loose. If we got wet, we got wet. A good dousing never killed children. Or adults. Many times, walking home from work, he would get caught in the rain. Instead of seeking cover, he would just walk on, come home soaked and Mother would fuss. There were times when I derived a certain pleasure from walking in the rain, too, got caught in a sudden downpour and would not take shelter. There was nothing perceptibly romantic about my father, but I liked to think that this streak, rare but thoroughly enjoyed, I got from him.

29

When Ramon and I graduated from the elementary school, our parents decided it was time we had a Catholic education. My sisters were already studying in Cebu, boarders at the *Colegio de la Inmaculada Concepcion,* but there were no boarding facilities for boys in the Catholic schools there. Our parents sent Ramon and me to a Catholic school in the city of Maasin, a few kilometers from our town. Here we lived in a house belonging to a cousin, Carmen. Here, too, other cousins boarded: Luisito, Belinda, and Carmela, children of our cousin, Luis.

Luis was an imposing man, tall and handsome, patrician in bearing, and moved with the self-confident manner of one born to great wealth. He married a woman whose family was noted for its beauty and they produced children whose extraordinary good looks were renowned in the province.

Luis' oldest daughter, Amanda, married another cousin, Manolo. Manolo managed the Maasin branch of his family's business, while his father, Don Manuel, took care of the main office in Cebu. Manolo installed his wife, Amanda, and their children in a house in the outskirts of town. Every Friday evening, he would take a ship from Maasin to Cebu to deliver reports and money to his father. He would come early and wait for the ship in Carmen's house where we stayed, which was near the pier. Here he spent the time in conversation with his wife's brother, Luisito, and his wife's two younger sisters, Belinda and Carmela, with Carmen's sons, and with Ramon and me.

"Manolo is going to teach me how to drive," Belinda informed us happily one afternoon. She had, as did the other women in her family, a most exquisite face, with green eyes that sparkled when she was pleased. What a surfeit of beauty in every member of their family! It was as though it was Christmas when the genes of their parents were created, their Maker handing out presents soft-spun in

crystal stars, gift wrapped in moon gold, *here, stamp this code on
your genes, only beautiful people come from here.*

- - - -

One day, Manolo asked Ramon and me to come with Belinda,
Luisito and Carmela in his Packard. He was teaching Belinda to
drive. "After the driving lesson, we could go out for ice cream," he
said.

How easy it was to please me in those days. I liked ice cream a
little; I liked riding in the Packard a lot. The car was big and ran
smoothly. I was delighted to go. This was the beginning of many
more afternoons, of driving lessons that never reached fruition,
followed by ice cream. Sometimes we ventured farther, going to
the neighboring towns, for exotic suppers, and desserts more
exciting than ice cream.

Our role was to chaperone them, but as chaperones went, we
were not much. Manolo was, after all, a much older cousin, and he
was married to Belinda's older sister. Although we always thought
him pompous and stuck up, pompous and stuck up we could
tolerate if we did not get them in large doses. So we mostly paid no
heed to his swagger and his affected pronouncements. We had
been exposed to his overbearing views since we were children,
listened to him without hearing, let his words bounce outside our
consciousness, learned to dismiss him---*he's just a humbug.*

So we did not mind him much as we chattered among
ourselves. I, not difficult to please, enjoyed the drive, relished the
food, tried not to notice his hands that could not seem to leave
Belinda alone. Later, when we definitely could not ignore the
dance of seduction whose beat was shooting sparks through the
roof right under our noses, I stifled whatever feelings of culpability
I felt with my usual defense: I was just a kid, the youngest of us
all, let the older ones act on it. Expectedly, Ramon did. This
frightening lack of caution concerned him, even if it did not seem
to concern Belinda's brother and sister.

Belinda had an air of childlike innocence about her that one
could not think her capable of doing anything sinful, much less
anything sexually sinful, and we were even younger. But Ramon

must have his say. As I said, Ramon always spoke what was on his mind, even if it meant putting his foot in his mouth, which he did often.

"You do not have to sit on his lap when he's teaching you to drive," Ramon reproved Belinda after one of these driving lessons. "You'd learn faster if you're seated comfortably in front of the steering wheel."

"You really think so?" said Belinda, looking at us with those glass-green eyes, batting long eyelashes, innocence personified. "But Manolo said it's better that way. I could run over somebody, you know, holding the wheel on my own, he said." Looking at my brother's glowering face, she soothed him with that heart-stopping smile. "Oh, Mon, we must trust Manolo in these things. After all, he is older than we are."

There it was, the older-means-wiser cliché that I never agreed with, especially not now, seeing older in such a stealthily sinister and dangerously reckless light.

"You had to speak," I said to my brother later.

"Aw, shut up," answered my brother irritably, brows furrowed in a worried frown. Belinda was, after all, a cousin for whom we cared very much; her family was very close to our hearts. We had much cause for concern.

A local doctor, Doctor John, had been interested in Belinda for quite some time. I had often wondered why she never returned his affections. He was one of the best doctors in the province, and cut quite a dashing figure about town. He was not, by a long shot, as good-looking as any member of Belinda's family. But then, nobody was. But Doctor John, on his own, was quite a catch: sophisticated, articulate, accomplished in his profession, and very commanding, which I thought went well with Belinda's reticence.

Sometimes, local fishermen would use dynamite to catch fish. Doctor John had been adamantly against it, as well he should. "You would get hurt, the dynamite could explode in your hand, dynamite is a blight to the fishing industry, you're also killing the small fish, one of these days there won't be any fish left to catch," etcetera, etcetera. Of course there was always someone deaf to his lectures.

One day, one patient told him that a fisherman had gone out and used dynamite again. "The catch was very good, Doctor, in fact there's a lot of fish in the market right now."

Doctor John went to the marketplace with a bottle of *fenecada*, that foul-smelling disinfectant that they used in hospitals to take care of the more tenacious germs that *Lysol* could not scare.

"All right, all right," he asked around, "where is this fish that just met dynamite?"

"Over there, Doctor, over there." The townspeople were just too eager to tell.

He went over there, poured this thick, vile stuff on the fish spread out on the slab of cement, rendering the fish beyond redemption, and the marketplace smelling like a hospital ward for days.

Once, a fisherman blew off part of his hand with the dynamite he used. The hand had to be amputated or gangrene would set in, Doctor John said. When the fisherman objected, Doctor John whipped out his gun. "I either cut your hand or I blow you out to kingdom come. Either way, you will be out of your misery. Now, which one is it?"

I guess he just came on too strong for Belinda, sweet, soft, heartbreakingly naïve Belinda, losing her way in front of our helpless eyes.

-     -   -   -

One weekend when we came home, my brother followed Father to his room. "Papa, may I talk to you?" At times when I felt that something momentous was going to happen that was none of my business, I attempted the art that my brother was so good at: I lurked in the corner, trying to be invisible, my ears wide open.

Father motioned to my brother to come in. "What is it?" asked Father, sitting down on the bed. Ramon began tentatively. "The other night in Carmen's house, I woke up to go to the bathroom."

"Yes," Father prompted.

"You know I have to pass the girls' room to reach the bathroom." He hesitated.

Father looked at Ramon and squinted. He looked as if he knew this conversation did not bode well. "Yes, well?" he said, his voice an octave lower than usual.

"Manolo was in bed with Belinda," Ramon said swiftly, relieved to have this out of his heart, which must have throbbed in great distress, and into someone else's.

"Ramon," Father shot out of the bed on where he was sitting. "That is a bad, bad thing to say. You see something and you give it a different meaning. You are too young; you don't know what you are talking about. Belinda is too good to let anything like that happen." He went on some more, very agitated, chafing on this same vein. I was sure that Ramon, for once, was sorry he opened his mouth. "I never, never want you to say that again, do you hear? Never ever again."

With the magnitude, the enormity of this information too appalling for him to even contemplate, Father's first instinct was to silence it out of existence, don't think about it, don't look at it too deeply, let your thoughts and your looks bounce off it, and mercifully, it will go away.

"There, I should have kept that to myself," Ramon said.

"Well, as Papa always says, *basta con la intencion,*" I consoled him.

"What intentions," grumbled my brother as he glared at me.

"The good ones that pave the road to wherever," I muttered.

Had Father not erupted too soon, Ramon would have blurted out another piece of indigestible information for him. The servants in Carmen's house who cleaned our rooms found pills on Belinda's bed and gave them to Carmen's sons. "Let's go and ask Doctor John what these are for." We forthwith marched to the doctor's office.

"Where did you get these?" Doctor John inquired.

"On one of the beds at home. What are they, Doctor?" asked one of Carmen's sons.

"These are Belinda's, right?" He looked very angry, the skin between his brows creased with vertical lines. We dared not answer and just nodded mutely. "I had suspected this," he said, shaking his head.

"What are they for, Doctor?"

"These are what evil men give to girls when they want to do evil things to them. Here, let's get rid of them, boys."

This information would surely have sent Father crashing clear through the ceiling.

Father usually attacked a problem when it presented itself and brought it to a swift resolution, but with this one, he staggered with the weight, the sheer contemptibleness of it. How could he bear this bitter information to Belinda's parents? But how could he not? And Ramon. He most certainly would bear the brunt of the savage accusations in the upheaval that undoubtedly would follow. It would have been easier not to believe Ramon. After all, it was late at night, the room was dark. Father did not have a high opinion of Manolo; he believed him capable of a lot of dastardly acts, but this one was just more reprehensible than any acts he could imagine. But he knew Ramon did not lie. Ramon listened to gossip, transported it to other ears, but he did not generate gossip, nor embroider it. And he did not lie. Of my parent's children, I was the only one who could lie without thinking twice about it. All my sisters could not tell a lie to save themselves.

Take Juanita, for example. One time when she was little and got sick, Father asked her. "Did you take your pill?" She did not answer. She just looked up at him, guilt written on her face. "Did you?" Father persisted. "No," she said under her breath. "Where is it?" Father asked. "I spat it out the window," she replied. "Very well," said Father. He fetched a glass of water and the bottle of pills, took one out, and gave it to her. "You have to take your medicine," he said. "I cannot, Papa," she said. "You cannot? Well, there's something you can," Father said, "you can take your medicine now, or you can get a spanking first, then you can take your medicine after. Now, which is it going to be?" The spanking she had had, a medicine emotionally harder to swallow.

Some lessons were difficult, some not so, but Father taught them early and well. And so his children inherited his uncompromising values, lived his standards, walked in his footsteps, and almost always (I, alone, answered to the almost) filled his large shoes.

Ramon was just as upright. Could it be perhaps he had misunderstood? Because if he had not, then there would be sorrow too heavy for Father's heart to bear, and he would have to tell Belinda's father and break his heart, too. Would that the painful truth could be left to wither on the vine. Who else knew? If things had progressed this far, surely others must have noticed, and commented? This angel of a girl who looked as though she could not hurt a fly, could not put a dog out on a bad night, could not do those other things we believe angels could never do, could she shatter a marriage, her own sister's, no less? An abundance of beauty, held loosely by a flimsy thread of character, wavering in moments of temptation. Wavering? More like trancelike surrender, helpless oblivion, *here, take me, heaven can lash down its judgment later.*

While Father deliberated on his course of action, Manolo took things into his hands and the scandal erupted with thunderous proportions.

-    -   -   -

The nuns in the school asked Belinda to run for school muse. Since this was one of the many ways that nuns raised money for their many causes, Belinda consented. There were four or five other candidates, and the girl who put up the most money won. Manolo put down more money than that raised by all the other girls combined. There was no contest. Belinda won.

The dress for the big night had to be made by the best couturier in Cebu, of course. With their trust in Manolo---cousin, brother-in-law, husband---absolute, the family did not see anything improper in Manolo going with Belinda to Cebu for the fittings. At any rate, another cousin, Marina, chaperoned them.

Manolo checked Belinda and Marina into a hotel, and while Marina prepared herself for a long day in the city, Manolo said he and Belinda were going out for a bit of shopping and would be back for her. Marina waited and waited but still they did not come back. While she fretted, she noticed Manolo's suitcase standing in the closet. She opened it, she said, and looked inside. There, among papers in the side compartment, she found airplane tickets, for a country in Europe, I could not now recall where.

She broke out in a sweat, at a loss for what to do. They were coming back to the hotel, she was sure, since the tickets were still there. Maybe they'd wait until she had to do some business of her own, then they'd pack up and leave. Better bring the matter to one who had more authority.

She hurried to the house of Manolo's father, Don Manuel, and told him what she found. She could hardly describe the emotional uproar that followed. Manolo's mother, Isabel, was beside herself with rage, and abused Belinda in no uncertain terms. When her anger had subsided to a degree where she could breathe easier, Don Manuel sent out his people to search for the errant pair. Meanwhile they sent word to Belinda's father, Luis, to come to Cebu.

The sight of Luis, accompanied by two of his sons, again raised Isabel's temperature to fever pitch. She put the blame on him for not watching over his daughter, instead of putting the blame on her son, who was married to Belinda's sister, who was very much older than Belinda, and should have been more responsible.

When the couple was found and brought to his presence, Luis told Manolo in no uncertain terms that he better not present himself again in Leyte. Then they whisked Belinda home.

A day later, Manolo was back, but instead of going home to his wife, Amanda, he went to Carmen's house. He sent one of Carmen's sons to ask Amanda to come, as he wanted to discuss this matter with her. Why he wanted to talk over his personal affairs in Carmen's house instead of his own we never were able to fathom. But after what he did to Belinda, nothing he would do could surprise us.

Amanda arrived at Carmen's house, composed in grave distress, that great beauty gathered inside herself. To give them privacy, we went out of the room, but not out of hearing distance. We grouped together, in silence, in the next room.

"I have asked you to come," Manolo started, "because I cannot go on living with you anymore. I have fallen in love with your sister. I am very sorry." Short, succinct, a dagger straight to the heart.

"If that's what you want," Amanda answered, her voice clear and even. She had always been very sweet, very retiring, but if we expected her to break down, we were very wrong. "If that's what you want, there's nothing I can do. Now if you don't have anything more to say, I'd like to go home." Just like that! She handled herself with such grace our hearts broke for her. But then she had always been one class act, a cousin to be proud of. As for Manolo, all we could say was that he was not.

He sent his driver for a bottle of Fundador and soothed his sorrows in brandy, all night, in the living room of Carmen's house. The Fundador drowned what sense of propriety he had left in him, and loosened his restraint and his tongue as well. "*O, Belinda, mi amor, me voy a morir,*" he lamented between guzzles of brandy. Oh, Belinda, my love, I am going to die. And other idiotic declarations like that.

At one point, interrupting himself, he went to one corner of the room where his suitcase stood and took out a valise behind it. "Take care of this, will you?" he said. He opened the valise. It was filled with money. I had never seen a five-hundred bill in my life, much less packs of them arranged neatly in stacks, filling every space of the suitcase. How many five-hundred bills could a valise like this hold? Smart with figures as I prided myself I was in those days, the amount here boggled my mind.

He took out one wad, held together by a strip of paper in the middle, looking as though it just came out fresh from the bank, and handed it to us. "Here, hold this for me for safekeeping. Keep some, too, for your needs." Money from his father's company to buy abaca, no doubt. Don Manuel certainly had a lot of paying up to do.

"No, no, thanks, you keep it, keep it," we declined as one, "there is really nothing we need."

For days he stayed in the living room of Carmen's house, drinking his head off, lamenting his sad fate. Then, too intoxicated for dignity, he instructed his driver to drive him to Luis' house. By this time, of course, rumors of the affair had already spread in town like wildfire.

Banned entrance to Luis' house, he stood on the street, under the window, crying the same lament, "*O, Belinda, mi amor, me voy a morir.*"

The people inside the house carried their stoic selves like silent shadows, while the people outside stood gripped by the events, and for days breathed, ate, drank, talked of nothing else.

What emotional support her family gave Amanda, who needed it the most, we never knew. As close a family as we were, some matters were too delicate to comment on or inquire about. We had perfected the art of looking without seeing, listening without hearing, hoping that bad things, if ignored, would go away. And so we turned our heads the other way and again told ourselves, *This too shall pass.*

The town had never witnessed drama as high, theater as enthralling, scandal as delicious. In our house we moved like ghosts, as though anguish as heavy as death had touched us. I had not seen Father so despairing. We did not talk about the affair, and drained by the intensity with which the affair had consumed us, I, at least, did not hear my parents talk about it, either.

The years passed. Manolo reconciled with Amanda, prompting the people of the town to pronounce: *The procession always goes back to church,* and other such inanities. He moved his family to Cebu, and never set foot in town again. Amanda never forgave Belinda, and as far as we knew, never saw her again. As for the other members of their family, they held their heads high, retreated to their hurt selves, explained neither sin nor sinner. And the years passed and with them the injury that the affair had dealt them.

-      -   -   -

We graduated from high school without any notable accomplishment, no honors, no medals, no awards, just an unexceptional finish to four years of unenthusiastic scholarship. After graduation, Ramon told our parents he wanted to become a harbor pilot and wanted to apprentice in the harbor pilot school in Cebu.

"Why not just apprentice in one of the *L. Escaño* ships?" Mother said. Ramon did.

Emiliana and Clotilde were already in Manila, studying at the University of Santo Tomas. Then my turn came and it was off to Manila for me, too, to study mechanical engineering at the Mapua Institute of Technology.

30

College was not as exciting as I had pictured it would be. True, I had a certain amount of freedom now that I was away from home, but with cunning, I had always had a fair amount of freedom at home. Now I was always out of money and that made a lot of difference. My parents paid for room and board and the dormitory gave me breakfast and supper, meager meals compared to what I was used to at home. Mother was not about to finance my vices and so gave me an allowance barely enough to cover the bare necessities---fare to and from school, a bottle of soda and a sandwich for lunch, a little left over for snacks. But bare necessities were not what my life was about. Mother's idea of necessities greatly differed from mine, so I stripped that bare so as to finance *my* necessities, which included smoke, drink, and a movie now and then.

My parents believed that poverty was the strongest tool of discipline now that we were too big for the rod, and they never indulged us with trappings of extravagance. Besides, there were four of us studying in Manila at that time, and our parents could hardly afford bigger allowances. Emiliana and Clotilde were at the University of Santo Tomas; Ramon had come to take up Agriculture at Araneta University, and I was over at Mapua studying to be an engineer.

I could always depend on Clotilde for a few bucks when I was broke, and I was always broke.

Clotilde seldom ventured out of the dormitory where she and Emiliana stayed, did not relish shopping nearly as much as Emiliana did, so she never ran out of money. With some effort, I could arrange my thin face to look hungry and I could separate Emiliana from her shopping money, but with Clotilde, all I had to do was show and I would leave with a few bills in my hands.

Most times, I would walk from my boarding house to school, to have a little extra money for a cigarette. Ah, how I inhaled in those days! For a smoke I did walk a mile. But not for imported cigarettes. For those I would have to do more miles, and thin as I was, lugging my drawing board, after more than a mile I would have been dead. The domestic cigarettes had to suffice. For the once-in-a-while imported ones, we had to have girlfriends who vended cigarettes, and these we had; they were good for a couple of sticks, which lasted us till we got to school. We had different girlfriends who bartended, to stand us for a couple of drinks. And different girlfriends who worked in different movie houses, to let us in without paying. Of course in those days, girlfriends were friends who were girls, most times, not necessarily more than that.

Manila conducted business in strange ways those days. The first-class movie houses featured one movie. The cheaper ones, in suspicious neighborhoods, had double features, and the cheapest movie houses, located in the seediest part of town, had triple features. Sometimes, on very broke days, I ended up watching three movies in one afternoon, and came out of the movie house dizzy and cross-eyed.

Ah, the travails of becoming an engineer were not the engineering courses, but the extracurriculars that had to be hurdled with so much effort.

-     -   -   -

On vacations from school, I worked with *L. Escaño* and often served as *Tio* Lorenzo's driver. At times I had to drive him to Maasin and this was the part of my work that I liked best. When one was young, the main pleasure of driving was driving fast. At first my sisters objected to the way I drove. "If you're flying, you're flying too slow," they complained. But sarcasm was wasted on me. I would fly slower still, letting the jeep crawl so that people walking the streets could catch up with us. My sisters stopped complaining and gave up.

But I had a lot of practice.

I learned to drive before I was nine years old, much too small to see through the windshield of the six-by-six trucks that were used to transport abaca, my legs still too short to reach the pedals.

From school, I would race to Father's office and hang about with the drivers in the grounds of the warehouse where the trucks were parked, hoping to be asked to help. When a truck needed to be moved, a driver would look at me and say, "Want to move it?"

I would clamber up the truck eagerly, slide down to reach the pedals, stick my head out the side of the truck to see where I was going, sometimes driving the truck outside the warehouse grounds. It must have been a curious sight---a six-by-six truck rolling down the road, seemingly with nobody at the wheel.

-     -   -   -

Once, a priest from across the bay came to visit and asked Mother. "And where is that son of yours who used to take wings when he drove, scattering leaves and debris all over the road when he passed?"

My poor mother! If she was not taken to task for that son who was too overly fond of the bottle, she was made to account for him whose reputation for driving like the wind had crossed the bay as well. I hoped that in moments like these, she consoled herself with the thought that she did not do too poorly. Her other son could not be faulted, and neither could her daughters. One in six could not be that much of a disaster.

But *Tio* Lorenzo did not mind my speed at all, and in fact thought that that was the way to go, the jeep lapping up the kilometers with speeds that swept the country roads of leaves and litter. At each town we passed, he would look at his watch and say, "We're making good time." An uncle after my own heart.

Tio Lorenzo's exacting standards, which demanded nothing less than perfection, often got his employees, and even his family, in trouble. My sister Juanita and I were probably two of the very few people who worked for *L. Escaño* who never got scolded by *Tio* Lorenzo. Emiliana didn't either, using alertness and cunning. On vacations, she also worked as timekeeper for *L. Escaño* and as gofer for *Tio* Lorenzo. When she saw the dark clouds of bad temper hover over *Tio* Lorenzo's head, she would get herself as far out of his way as ingenuity could get her.

Tio Lorenzo would look for her. "Where's Lily?" That was her nickname, Lily. She was born on the 8th of February, the feast of *Nuestra Senora de los Lirios,* Our Lady of the Lilies. The drivers would cover for her. "She was here just a minute ago," one of them would say, "let me go look for her," grateful for an excuse to get as far away from *Tio* Lorenzo as possible. After *Tio* Lorenzo had chewed somebody out and the clouds had passed, Lily would appear before him, all innocence. "You looked for me, *Tio*?"

Emiliana! She had her moments, too. Once, her report card arrived; she got a grade of *75*. This caused quite a hue and cry in the family. Barely passing was barely acceptable. She was very bright. This was the first time she had fallen low; since nobody expected it, it caused quite a stir. *Tio* Agustin called on my parents.

"Ced," *Tio* Agustin said to Mother, "we must have a party for Lily. You know, Ced," *Tio* Agustin continued, "*75* is a very hard number to get. Not just *74*, mind you, not *76* either, but exactly on target, *75*."

Perhaps that was one reason she had a soft spot in her heart for me. She understood that there were times when one's moments could get out of hand, when, though not thinking to cause grief, by just not thinking at all, one did.

She liked taking care of me. From the time when we were small, she took care of Clotilde, Ramon and me and when Mama had to go somewhere and could not take us, she played mother to us.

One day Mother was away and there they were, making bets on who could blow the biggest bubble from their bubble gum. Mother had a rule on this: I was never, ever, to be given bubble gum, lest I suck it in instead of blow it out, and choke to death.

There I was, a thin six-year-old, looking at Emiliana with puppy eyes, gazing longingly at the pink bubbles coming out of their mouths from the forbidden bubble gum.

She melted, as I knew she would. "Oh, all right," she said, "but be careful you don't swallow it."

I put the gum in my mouth, chomped on it happily, blew a bubble, and faster than they could say *don't*, inhaled and swallowed it. I gasped for breath, got blue in the face, thought I would die. My sisters were frantic, thought of Mother, and knew they were dead. Emiliana rushed, got white in the face, made me drink kerosene. I sputtered and spat and coughed out air and sprays of kerosene and out flew the killer gum.

"Don't tell Mama, all right?" they cautioned me when it was all over.

"All right," I said meekly, too exhausted to quibble after my near-death experience.

"If you tell, we shall never let you play with us again. Understand?"

"Yes."

"You won't forget?"

"No."

When Mother entered the gate, I rushed to her. "Mama, Mama, they gave me bubble gum. It got stuck in my throat and I could not breathe for a long time. Then they made me drink kerosene. Jeezus, Mama, they almost killed me."

-    -   -   -

Emiliana was my champion. If anybody bullied me, he had her to contend with. I came home once, clothes dirtied and nose bloodied, from a fight with a son of a neighbor. Quietly, Emiliana sought him out.

"Next time you touch my brother, you deal with me," she warned.

Bloodied noses did not bow my head; having my sister take up my fights for me did.

She was a wisp of a girl, shorter than my other sisters, and just as thin, but she had the family trait of speaking her mind and standing her ground. She had a fearless air about her that awed even the bullies of our town.

Once, coming down from a ship in Manila, she had an argument with a porter working the pier. "Oh," the man cursed, "your mother is a bitch," a loose translation of the Spanish-Filipino he actually used. He was the kind of man who would use those curse words if he accidentally dropped a coin, say, or bumped into a chair in the dark, or received a check from a long-lost uncle. But of course Emiliana did not know that. We come from the Visayan-speaking part of the Philippines. The medium of instruction in schools was English; at home we spoke either the Visayan dialect or English or Spanish, what lessons in the national language we learned in school did not prepare us for conversational Tagalog. My sisters did not go to Tagalog movies, were exposed to conversational Tagalog only when they went to college in Manila. They therefore were not prepared for the Tagalog curses peppered liberally with Spanish words that would have made Mother clean their mouths with soap if they uttered such words in the house. Emiliana therefore did not know that many Filipinos used that curse phrase as a matter of course, whether they worked in the pier or in some levels higher than that. Or know that people began and ended sentences with it, inserted it into the middle, used it as a complete sentence, as an adjective, as an exclamation, in disbelief. *Your mother is a bitch.* In this country, that was used as parsley, to flavor sentences, color remarks.

"How dare you insult my mother!" Emiliana stormed and swung her handbag, catching the man squarely on the face. Juanita pulled her away before the stunned man realized what hit him.

"Are you crazy?" Juanita was very angry. "He could have picked you up and thrown you into the water and would not have thought twice about it."

But Emiliana must speak her mind and stand her ground, and, in this case, fell the adversary with her handbag.

31

Tio Agustin, *Tio* Lorenzo and *Tia* Piling were all lovers of music and even before the War, had lent their patronage to several musical plays presented in Cebu City. Every other year or so, my sisters and cousins and the other young people in our town mounted musicals and presented them in the theater that *Tio* Agustin had built near the villa. We had a good team there: *Tio* Agustin, the artist, did the sets himself. *Tio* Lorenzo and *Tia* Piling produced the plays, attended rehearsals, and gave artistic critiques. Some of the plays were in English, some were in Spanish, some were translated from English and Spanish into the local dialect. We always had a full house. Even people from the mountain barrios came down and they always had a thoroughly enjoyable time, although sometimes these events were just over their heads. We presented an operetta once, in English. Afterwards, one man was asked how he liked it. "I just loved it," he enthused, "although I did not understand the story. You know, I don't speak Spanish

- - - -

All Jacinto Aberásturi's children could carry a tune well. Tina's soprano was very good; after she studied Music at Santa Escolastica in Manila it became even better.

For her recital, Jacinto chartered The Aristocrat, at that time one of the most elegant and expensive places in Manila, and engaged the entire Philippine Philharmonic Orchestra. "Wow, how's that for affluence!" I marveled when I heard about it.

The youngest son, Jacinto Junior, had such a lovely tenor that one of the treats for me, and for everybody in our town, was listening to his voice at weddings of family members, or at church affairs when he could be persuaded to sing, which, sad to say, was not often. He could not deny *Tio* Lorenzo, however, and could never say no to the much loved *Tio* Agustin; either of them could prevail upon him to sing, albeit reluctantly, in plays. He shied at being the center of attention, for when that voice floated over and filled the theater or the church with exquisite loveliness, gliding smoothly into the high notes instead of assaulting them, the thrilled listener was no longer connected to the outside world but was entranced by that voice. And that face. Unlike other singers whose faces distorted, with eyes bugging out while attacking the high register, Jacinto's handsome face stayed unruffled, his blue eyes calm. When he was in college at San Beda in Manila, he once sang and so impressed Mrs. Kahn, one of Manila's social arbiters and foremost patron of the arts, that she immediately offered him a job with San Miguel Beer, where her husband was one of the company big shots, if he would stay in Manila and let her be his mentor, let her guide his career. I often wondered what heights he might have reached had he stayed, but he did not wish to. Like his other family-bound brothers and sisters, he just had a great longing for home---for his family, his town, a small-town life. As his parents provided their children with more than enough for their tangible, and sometimes even their intangible needs, he did not yearn for more.

   Tio Lorenzo's children, Juan, Nenita and the youngest, Bingo, were all excellent at the piano. One fond memory is of Juan, accompanying himself on the piano, as he sang a Cole Porter song, *In The Still Of The Night.* Or that song that recalled the loneliness of war, *I'll Be Seeing You.*

   When we presented a play, Nenita directed and accompanied on the piano. Juan sang with Juanita, who shared directorial tasks with Nenita, and Emiliana choreographed. Mostly, the plays were musicals; operettas of Franz Lehar's or Victor Herbert's or other giants of the operetta world that *Tio* Lorenzo, *Tia* Piling, and Mother so loved. The principals were often Juan and Juanita. Juanita's voice could soar as high as the highest notes the operettas demanded, and Juan's tenor was just as excellent, so we never had a problem there. And when she was in town, there was Tina Aberásturi, effortless in *Italian Street Song*, like Jeanette MacDonald in *Naughty Marietta.* And she was more beautiful, without question.

Cousins, nieces, nephews and several young people of the town made up an admirable ensemble, rehearsals gave us another reason to get together, and the plays offered a break from the humdrum of daily living. On play nights, everyone in town, and even those from out of town, came, especially since admission was very cheap. We always had a full house.

Romances bloomed and withered while we prepared for these plays.

Otic Escaño fell in love with Inday Arevalo, *Tia* Piling's niece. As with the other children of Doctor Arevalo, Inday went to the best schools in Cebu, was excellent at the piano, and was an accomplished singer.

Otic Escaño was in love with Inday Arevalo long before we hatched the idea of presenting plays, but his love certainly blossomed during rehearsals. As garrulous as he was when fueled with drink, when it came to matters of his heart, Otic's tongue was tied. He would gaze at Inday's lovely face, and just freeze. She had the loveliest eyes, and when they glanced his way, Otic was a goner. He took care of his other cousins' love life, stood in *Tio* Agustin's stead when Emit needed to take care of his, but Otic's feelings for Inday found no voice. The fuller his heart, the more mute his tongue.

Frustrated that he could not express how he felt, he would pretend to us that there was something going on between them, although we knew better. When at parties she ignored him, he would say, "There she goes, mad at me again." He invited her to dinner; she accepted once, but subsequently declined. He sent her gifts; finding expression in offerings that he could not find in his silent suit; the more bothered he was, the more exaggerated the gift; a whole roast pig once, which of course she promptly sent back. After all, he had not yet declared his intentions. Would she have been less impervious to his distress and looked more kindly on him had he been less dumb? Maybe not. The Arevalo children leaned more to the spiritual than to the worldly side of life. Three brothers entered the priesthood; three sisters became nuns. After a while, Inday got herself to the nunnery. This was serious business; we felt bad for Otic. We turned our heads the other way and for a while desisted from mentioning the subject of nunneries in his presence.

I had a girlfriend here once, too, a state of affair that also flourished while we were rehearsing for one of these plays. But that thing did not thrive too well. I was not for her. She fell in love with Mely Sala, silent, introspective Mely Sala. As I said, Mely's quiet bearing appealed to the romantic fancies of the ladies. It certainly appealed to Mary Oben's, as well. That was that for that romantic interlude.

The vast cast of plays such as *The King and I* and *Oklahoma* never posed a problem, presented as they were in the summer, when a swarm of nephews and nieces was home from school.

Mini, translated to the dialect, was an extraordinary play, with a cast that included a *carabao*, the Filipino water buffalo, our chief beast of burden. Otic Escaño and Juan Escaño and the other cousins and nephews, and of course I, as well, with my nondescript tenor, outdid ourselves when the play opened that night. The drinking started early and spirits rose long before the curtains did. The *carabao*, being a member of the cast, imbibed a good deal, too, straight from a pail that Otic Escaño, at that time of day already in his high-spirited elements, placed under its nose. But not being a member of the distinguished Drinkers Club, the *carabao* did not know how to hold its drink as the strange brew rumbled in its insides. It was a noteworthy debut: the *carabao* discharged its troublesome cargo, a great vile, foul pile, right there in the middle of the stage, causing consternation on my sisters' part and uncontainable laughter on everybody else's. Needless to say, it was a riot of a play. Juanita and Emiliana did not talk to us for days after that.

Other plays were not as wild, practice was as enjoyable as the actual presentation, and except for the drinking, or maybe because of it, the shows were always memorable events.

32

Bribery was the lifeblood of most businesses in the country. This was especially more true in government matters. Travelers who came in from abroad clipped a few dollar bills inside their passports. This was a standard practice, safe because no bribe was blatantly offered. If the traveler got an honest custom official, which was almost an oxymoron in that part of the world, the bills were left untouched and taxes were imposed on the incoming luggage. Most times, the traveler got an official who could not support both the woman he had married, and the other woman he had on the side, on the salary the government paid him, or an official who had developed a taste more expensive than what he could afford, or one who, through the years, had justified his cheating on the excuse that everybody did it, anyway. One's conscience could get callused when constantly rubbed with excuses. After a while these officials had gotten used to these underhanded practices that they no longer had to lower their eyes in shame at the whole disgraceful state of affairs. Then the bills were removed from the passport without comment, the luggage was initialed without inspection, and the wise traveler justified his part, too, in corrupting a public servant: bribery was alive and well in this part of the world.

Sometimes, though, when yonder moon turned blue, the customs official got a difficult customer, one who seemed not to understand how these things were done, who stood in front of him tapping her heels, fanning herself impatiently.

"You know, Ma'am," the custom official informed Cristina, "we could make this easy for you." He certainly could. Cesar and Cristina and their family traveled abroad almost every year. But Cesar and Cristina were a match. The road to their heaven must not be paved by a leech who was waiting without shame for his booty.

"No, no, no," my sister answered brusquely, as though wanting to do her part in eradicating vermin, "I don't want you to make it easy for me. Levy the taxes now. Then you give me the receipt and I shall pay you the money." A daughter of her father, too.

                    -      -   -   -

Bribery thrived in public offices, too. Vouchers for payment were signed and dispatched more quickly if accompanied by invitations to lunch, perhaps, or gallons of ice cream for the group, or small gifts, such as jars of imported tea or coffee for the entire group, not obtrusive enough to take away dignity or self-respect, but effective enough to hasten one's agenda.

Tio Lorenzo and Father, though, were of a different breed, born at a time long ago, when right was still might, but they had to go to great lengths to make it so.

Abaca bales had to pass inspection by the town fiber inspectors. Fiber inspectors, however, came and went quickly, and sometimes, new ones would come who were not warned about how Father worked. They would try the familiar rigmarole.

"*Señor* Dioni," the fiber inspector would say, "this bale could not pass inspection." He hoped Father, to save time and energy, would yield, and favors would change hands. They were not told that this exercise had been tried and tested before, and failed.

"Is that so?" said Father. They exchanged arguments across the table for a while. "All right," Father said, "give me a sample of the fiber that failed inspection, write down how you arrived at your conclusion, put your signature on it, and I shall bring it to the regional inspector."

This would take a lot of Father's time, but they would have died for their principles, Father and *Tio* Lorenzo, though death was not called for, just a lot of bother and time and effort, not to mention expense.

That night, Father and I boarded the ship to Cebu where the regional fiber inspection office was located. We had done this before: crossing the sea, wasting our hours, wasting his money.

After dealing in the abaca business for years, Father was already a familiar sight in the office of the regional fiber inspector. "But of course, *Señor* Dioni," the chief fiber inspector said, "your classification is right, as always. I shall personally ask for a meeting with the town fiber inspector."

Father was vindicated; the fibers were certified, he did not have to pay any bribe. We just squandered his own money, since he would never even think of charging *L. Escaño* for our expenses, official though our business in Cebu was. The money we spent was more than what the town fiber inspectors expected, anyway; but history is peopled with those who lost their lives in defense of their principles; all Father lost was one whole day. Although it was not his intention, he won the respect of the people he dealt with, even, I was sure, of the fiber inspectors in our town. He certainly won mine. There were times, many times, when Father looked very tall in my eyes.

-    -   -   -

The scourge of *Tio* Lorenzo's life were the Customs officers who went to so much effort to pry bribe money from him. Ramon's ambition to become a harbor pilot died because of *Tio* Lorenzo's principles.

From the time he was little, Ramon had wanted to become a harbor pilot. After high school, he wanted to train in Cebu, but Mother persuaded him to apprentice in one of the *L. Escaño* ships instead. There were, however, some things that one could not control in these ships.

Ships were allowed only a certain number of passengers to pass Customs inspection. If they carried more passengers than was deemed safe, Customs officers refused to give permission for the ship to depart. Usually, the *Jefe de Viaje*, the ship's purser, would oblige; money would change hands, a familiar Philippine song-and-dance, and the ship could leave. But *Tio* Lorenzo and Father never condoned bribery in any form, and they were never known to negotiate, so that the exchange of money for permission for the ships to leave port was never done when *Tio* Lorenzo was on board.

This time, however, through some oversight, *Tio* Lorenzo was aboard, fuming because it was already late and the ship was still at harbor. The ship, overloaded as usual, could not leave---too many passengers, Customs said. Customs was waiting for its money; *Tio* Lorenzo was unwittingly standing guard over his; the *Jefe de Viaje*'s hands were tied.

"It's late, why are we not leaving?" *Tio* Lorenzo asked, already very annoyed.

The thing to do in times like these was to be as far away from *Tio* Lorenzo as was possible, and let the *Jefe de Viaje*, whose job it was anyway, take care of matters, be fired for one night if need be, return to work again the next day. But Ramon did not see *Tio* Lorenzo coming his way. *Tio* Lorenzo saw him first and wanted answers. Ramon had none. At least none that he could give *Tio* Lorenzo. He could snitch, and tell *Tio* Lorenzo the facts of life on the *L. Escaño* ships, but a snitch he was not.

"Why are we not leaving?" *Tio* Lorenzo thundered again.

"There are just too many passengers, *Tio*," Ramon answered.

"Well, then, check the tickets of all the passengers and throw down all those without tickets," ordered *Tio* Lorenzo.

"I can't do that, *Tio*. They will never get off the ship," Ramon said. He was getting aggravated, too. People were watching, he was being scolded. He wanted to say, *Why don't you try it. Even you cannot make them get off once they are already on board.* But that would have been impertinent, and he had been raised better than that.

This was really not Ramon's duty, but *Tio* Lorenzo expected more from him and he could not deliver.

"You can't? You can't? Then you're just good for nothing." This happened all the time to other *L. Escaño* employees---the rebukes, even the firings, that *Tio* Lorenzo administered but never meant. These stories were amusing when later retold, if they happened to others and not to you. But Ramon had too much dignity to be amused. There were people around. He was deeply shamed. And so he fired himself.

He came home and had a long talk with Father. "Ramon," Father said patiently. "You know Lorenzo did not mean it. He never means it. Especially not with you."

"Well, he said I was good for nothing. I just can't let that pass. And really, Papa, you should not let people who are good for nothing work in your company." He was very upset. "Even he could not make those people get off the ship. I was extremely humiliated."

"Ramon," Father said, shaking his head, "think this over first."

"Papa, I have thought this over many times. I just don't want to work in your company anymore. I quit."

Father, seeing in this son the very Basque trait of not changing one's mind once it was made up, said wearily, "I wish you wouldn't. I know even Lorenzo won't want you to. But whatever you do, you know you have my support."

I thought of St. Ignatius Loyola, the founder of the Jesuits, of whom one companion remarked: "Remember, he is Basque, and once he had taken something to heart . . . "

Father went with Ramon to *Tio* Lorenzo's house.

"Ramon," said *Tio* Lorenzo, "You know I don't want you to resign." But there was nothing *Tio* Lorenzo could say to dissuade him. And so resign he did.

I would like to put down here that when Father died, *Tio* Lorenzo offered Father's job to Ramon, asked him to take Father's place in the company, but of course Ramon declined.

What went on between him and *Tio* Lorenzo was not mentioned again. My sisters did not even know what happened or why he left *L. Escaño*. He expunged that part of his life, maybe thought of sometimes but certainly not spoken of again. He canceled all aspirations of ever working in ships, or becoming a harbor pilot, or doing anything that had to do with the sea, ever again, and that was the last time he worked for anyone.

Sometimes I wondered if he had just enough of this thing called family, where members could hurt each other more grievously than others who did not share one's blood, and so he exiled himself far, far from home.

He went to Araneta University in Manila and earned a degree in Agriculture. When he graduated, Father had another talk with him.

"Ramon," Father said, "what is the best agricultural school in the world?"

"Cornell University in the States, I guess," Ramon answered, surprised.

"Well," said Father, "you prepare yourself. I'm sending you there."

"Papa, do you have any idea how much that would cost?"

"I do," replied Father. "I'll take care of it."

"No, Papa, I appreciate your offer, and I don't want to sound disrespectful, but no more schools for me."

Ramon was well aware, as we all were, how much a burden it was for our parents to send us all to college in Manila. Juanita even declined to go, and instead worked as secretary to *Tio* Lorenzo, in order to give our parents a bit of financial respite.

Ramon and Father batted this proposal for a while, but Father knew Ramon had made up his mind, and that was all there was to it.

"Very well," said Father. "You know that I'm always behind you in whatever you want to do. I will support you in whatever decisions you make."

Ramon went to Cagayan de Oro way down south in Mindanao, to the City of the River of Gold, where it was said golden opportunities flourished especially for someone as young, determined, driven and disciplined as he was.

He was his father's son. He buckled down to work with a workday that started before dawn and ended long after dusk. He planted hectares in Arabica coffee, raised a few hundred heads of cattle, and for his soul, planted more hectares in roses and other flowers, which also turned to gold when people from all over town came to gaze, and admire, and buy. He grew other fruits and vegetables, supplied beef, and what went on the table with it, to the markets of the city, expanded his business to restaurants and hotels in Manila, filled ships with cattle and crates of his produce. He traveled to Australia to buy more cattle to breed, to supply the demand. In the process he made himself a very wealthy man.

33

Most evenings when he was still alive, Father and Tio Lorenzo would play a game of dice called *burro*. Very often, Fernanding Escaño, Otic's brother, and one or other of their friends would join them.

Tonight, I was here in Father's place, as I had done since he was gone and when I was home.

It was an enjoyable game---a set of dice rolled out of a leather cup, with one player keeping scores---and a pleasant way to spend an evening. But more than the game, I liked being there, in Father's place. I enjoyed the talk and the repartees and the quick wit of *Tio* Lorenzo. And then, of course, there was *Tia* Piling, hovering about, making sure the servants replenished our food, and freshened our drinks.

I remember one night I was home and we played *burro* here.

The wind had started to blow when I left the house to drive to *Tio* Lorenzo's for another night of cards. Tonight, there were *Tio* Lorenzo, the judge of the town, and Fernanding Escaño, Otic's brother.

Within the hour, the wind had gusted, whipping outside, rattling the windows. But *Tio* Lorenzo's house was planted firmly by the best engineers in the province, was larger than *Tio* Agustin's very large villa, and was called The White House, for its color as much as for being the largest house in town, so that the gathering tumult outside did not alarm us much. The game prospered with much amusement, as usual, as the rejoinders flew fast.

I was looking at my cards when *Tio* Lorenzo called out, "Fernanding, what's wrong?"

Fernanding's head slumped to one side. I echoed *Tio* Lorenzo, "Fernanding, what's wrong?" When he did not respond, I touched his shoulder and his face fell to his chest. Now we were alarmed!

"Fernanding, Fernanding," said *Tio* Lorenzo, as though trying to wake him from sleep. But Fernanding just sat there, his eyes closed, his head on his chest, sat there very, very still. He couldn't be dead!

"All right," said *Tio* Lorenzo, "let's bring him to the bed, then we call the doctor." We carried him over to one of the guest rooms, weighing a ton for one so thin. God, don't let this be the literal dead weight.

The doctor came, examined him, and looked at us in disbelief. "He's dead!"

The house now bustled with activity. *Tia* Piling had called the other members of the family. Now they gathered in the living room, quiet in shock, whispering to each other, shaking their heads in disbelief. *Tio* Lorenzo gave orders to notify Fernanding's wife and children, and the rest of the family. Despite the weather, the house started to fill.

Fernanding lay there peacefully, while the wind and the rain clamored outside, shaking the windows, demanding to come in.

Oh, would that I could make my exit this way, silently, peacefully, without combat. But, oh, Fernanding, of all nights to die, you had to choose this turbulent one.

-      -   -   -

Tonight there was nothing to disturb the evening, the game proceeded without chaos, it was great to be with *Tio* Lorenzo again, great to be in Papa's place, great to be home.

34

There were many milestones in our lives while I was in college in Manila that I missed with regret.

I was away when my sister Juanita married an American named Roy Wonderly, an engineer on one of the foreign ships that came to our shores to pick up abaca and copra. They spent their honeymoon at the Manila Hotel. After they were married, he wanted to take her with him to the States, of course, but Mother objected vehemently. True, several family members, herself included, married foreigners, but they were *Spaniards*, and Spaniards were more kindred. After all, Father was one. But Americans, well, America was not Spain, where some family members still lived, whose language many family members spoke more comfortably and more often than even the local dialect.

America was too far, Mother declared, Americans were a different breed, my sister had been too sheltered to be exposed too soon to strange American winds. Maybe later. Roy stayed a few months a year in our house, each time hoping my sister would go back with him. Each time he boarded the ship, again without her. Maybe later.

Meanwhile, Juanita prepared for that later. She had towels, sheets, pillowcases and such things embroidered: she filled chests with them. She prepared clothes; she prepared money, prepared for the later that never came.

-   -   -   -

I was still in college when my sister Clotilde married Alfredo Asuncion, a civil engineer from Cebu. The church was filled with orchids from our garden and, because there were too many guests from Cebu, the wedding reception was held in *Tio* Agustin's villa. After the wedding, Clotilde's husband brought her with him to a small town way down south where he was the highway project engineer. There they lived until they had a baby, and another baby was on the way. Then she wrote that her husband, who went to America on a scholarship to study highway engineering, was assigned to supervise the construction of miles and miles of highways "from where to where." He did not want to leave my sister alone with a new baby coming. She asked if she could come and live with us until the baby came. My parents were more than happy to have her back. They sent me and another cousin to fetch her from Cabasalan, the small town in Mindanao where they lived, and bring her and her baby back to Malitbog. I was more than happy to go; I missed her and was excited to see the baby.

Mindanao is an island unto itself, a world apart from other Philippine islands, with a large Muslim population that doesn't consider itself Filipino. They speak a different language, have their own manner of worship and practice an entirely different religion, and they decline to eat pork, a Filipino staple. They are exempted from Philippine laws prohibiting polygamy and divorce. They definitely do not share the Western culture that the Christian-Filipinos inherited from the conquering Spaniards and Americans. Their women still wear the traditional long garments that their Christian counterparts, weaned on Western styles modeled on *Vogue* and other American and European fashion bibles, find cumbersome.

Every once in a while, Muslim Filipinos agitated to secede from the Philippines, create an independent Islamic state, have their own government, control their own lives. Each time the Philippine government patted their backs, stroked their heads, and soothed them with enticing government programs until they calmed down. Once it had cooled down the unrest, the government promptly turned its attention to other backs that needed patting, putting the Muslim problem on the shelf, until next time. Then once again the Muslims erupted into protests, sometimes sputtering, sometimes thundering, but they remained still there, their problems unresolved. Muslims and Christians remain discrete societies often in conflict with one another.

We took a ship to Zamboanga City, where we had to pass to get to Cabasalan. A long time ago in school, we learned a song:

Don't you go, don't you go to far Zamboanga. How true. It was way too far.

We arrived at a city that was bustling, crowded, noisy; restless people crowding about. Several men wore tunics and pajama-like pants and turbans over their heads, chewed betel nuts, showed stained teeth when they opened their mouths, spewed brown spit anywhere they pleased. Women in long dresses slung half-naked children on their hips, chattering unintelligible noises. From there, we boarded a bus with relief.

The roads were bumpy and dusty, the bus was overcrowded, the air redolent with sweat. After what seemed an eternity of a morning, the bus stopped and the driver went to a small shanty that called itself a diner. "How long are we stopping?" people wanted to know, but the driver was in no mood for social amenities before his meal, and growled something under his breath.

We waited outside in the blazing heat while he took his own sweet time inside. To cool off our bodies and our tempers, we strolled over to the bridge that spanned a wide river, where women and children were immersed in the water with their long dresses still on, bathing and washing themselves and their brightly-colored clothes, as though they believed that bathing and washing clothes separately was a waste of time. One woman bent forward, cupped her hands together, brought them up, dripping, to her mouth and gulped down her drink. Her thirst not quenched, her cupped hands went back to the water for another drink. She paused to look at something brown floating in the way of her hands that looked like a Milky Way chocolate bar, but I was two hundred percent sure was not. She brushed the *thing* away with her hand as though brushing away a bothersome insect and bent down again to finish her drink. *No, you don't, no, you don't*, I warned silently, *you know what that thing was!* But she did, take a long drink from the water that just a minute ago coddled the suspicious chocolate bar she had sent bobbing away with a wave of her hand. *Jeezus*, I said in disbelief.

After a long while, the driver came out of the shanty, full, thirst quenched, in a better mood, and back on the bus we went, lurching on our way.

We arrived at a little quay where we took a small riverboat to navigate a narrow waterway. This was the saving grace of our otherwise unpleasant journey, this slim boat cutting through the water, leaving foam frothing in its wake, the flapping of bird wings rising from the marshes to the blue skies above as the boat disturbed their rest, the only discord in the stillness. Repose at last after the din of that obstreperous, raucous city!

The boatman deposited us in a desolate place, with a small pier, a Caltex depot, dust everywhere, and nothing else. We were not expected, and were not met.

We asked for directions but we were not understood and were ignored. "I guess we walk," I said. We did, until we reached a highway. "Ah, now we know where we are," I said. Alfredo was the project engineer of the government engineering corps that was building a hundred-something-mile highway.

Cabasalan was a dreary little town. The highway engineers lived in a housing facility; rows of uniform, matchbox-sized houses provided by the government. We approached the first house on the row, asked for directions, and were pointed towards my sister's house.

She was happily surprised to see us, and ushered us inside. There were two small bedrooms, a small living room that also served as the dining room, a small kitchen, a small bathroom. Such a small place for such tall people. Alfredo was a big man and tall, and my sister, though slim, was also tall/.

She bustled about trying to make us comfortable. The house was cheerless and forlorn despite the curtains blowing in the breeze. Amidst this bleakness my sister stood radiant in her pregnancy, well lost to the world in this gray and shabby town.

Her stomach was big with the second baby, but otherwise she was still all long arms and long legs. Somehow, she never gained weight, never wrinkled, never seemed to have faded. Like my other sisters, she showed some white on her hair too soon. Maybe later it would turn completely silver, like Father's. But now, that was about all that had faded about her.

"This is Ines," she said. The baby in the crib looked at us, her brown eyes huge as a fawn's, laughed as she laughed. If a baby's face could take your breath away, this one took away mine. Alfredo came home, brought us to the plantation of a friend, where we demolished a platter of prawns and practically emptied a bottle of brandy.

-      -   -   -

Even when we were young, I liked my sister Clotilde a lot, that is, when she was not soaping or scrubbing me down with her long arms. The youngest of my sisters, she was the only sister left while Juanita and Emiliana were in the Lopezes' *hacienda* with Cristina.

She was what was called "a good daughter," did what she was supposed to do, excelled in school, never gave our parents any problems. A little like pliant Cristina, unlike spirited Juanita and Emiliana.

Like my other sisters, she was tall and slim and had a head of thick, wavy hair. She hated to sit still to have it cut, and it grew around her head like a halo, giving the impression that she was fragile and delicate, which was far from the truth. She was very competent, could do things one did not associate with girls. She climbed trees when she wanted fruits, and had been known to climb out of bedroom or bathroom windows to the garden below when we had guests in the living room she did not care to talk to.

Once, one of my sisters told her that Miguel, another cousin, was coming over for *merienda*, the afternoon snack of coffee, cakes or whatever the cook had cooked up. It seemed he had fallen in love with Clotilde and wanted to press his suit.

Miguel came, waited for my sister. When she appeared, he began some trivial sentence to soothe his nerves. "Good afternoon," he said. But there was no comfort from my sister. She did not even let him finish the sentence.

"Miguel," she interrupted, "I know why you are here. *Pues,* the answer is no." She then marched to her room and left Miguel with his mouth open in astonishment. This astonished us, too, listening outside the room, but we could not help ourselves as we doubled up in amusement: nobody expected such a sharp tongue on an otherwise gentle girl!

Poor Miguel! She was not for him. But no matter. He would have other exciting chances later. He got married and fell off the bed the first night of his honeymoon. At least that was what Otic Escaño swore happened, *"Cross my heart, hope to die, true story."*

Even when we were still little, we were accomplices in many things, Clotilde and I. She would wink at me and whisper, *"Un traguito?"* I never refused these invitations and we would disappear into the pantry and raid our father's bottles of wine. One *traguito* would lead to two shots, then three, maybe four, and we would come out of the pantry bleary-eyed and happy. No one could ever say that Father, *Tio* Lorenzo or *Tio* Agustin *loved* to drink. They had wine with meals, but this was a Spanish custom. The next generation's love affair with the bottle started early, in furtive forages into family pantries, from tentative sips of fermented drinks, to more resolute swigs of the distilled variation.

- - - -

That was one of the happiest times of Father's life, those few months when my sister and her daughter came home to stay with us. Father, who rose long before dawn, would take Ines from my sister and play with her while he had his coffee. Sometimes he walked to work with Ines propped up giddily on his shoulders, and people they passed would *oh* and *ah* at such a beautiful baby.

- - - -

Alfredo finished his stint with the Philippine government, and with some friends founded the Construction Development Corporation of the Philippines, the CDCP, which grew into one of the largest corporations in the country.

He knew how to make money, and knew how to spend it, too. He bought the newest cars, which he changed often into newer models. They traveled abroad just as often. He built my sister a big house, sold that and built her a bigger one, then sold that one, too. The houses kept getting bigger, their locations pricier. But the craving for the simple and the uncomplicated was handed down to my sister by my mother like some genetic code. The bigger and more luxurious the houses, the more my sister's head ached. Swimming pools were the scourge of her life, this girl who lived her young life in spitting distance from water, but did not even relish swimming there.

"Wow!" we would marvel, each time we visited a new house bigger than the last, "this is almost a palace."

"Ay," she would snort, dismissing the house, "too big, too tiring, too much." She would recall fondly their first house in a less posh subdivision: small, easy to care for, did not need a pack of servants to maintain. "That was not a bad house," she reminisced wistfully. "Hey, we had Kokoy Romualdez there for a neighbor." Yeah, I remember him. Imelda Marcos' brother. Though she was not yet *the* Imelda Marcos of fable then, and she had not yet bestowed on this brother the Marcos magic power wand that could part the Philippine seas. Kokoy's wife belonged to the rich Gomez family, and when he drove through the neighborhood in their MG, neighbors would snicker and say, "MG! Mr. Gomez."

I always thought of Mother as the wellspring of frugality from where my sister must have taken a long drink. To save on gas, Clotilde would open the windows of her car rather than switch on the air conditioner, and come home with her nose all smudged with the smoke that the other vehicles in front of hers had belched.

Like most Filipino women when they were expecting, my sister craved fruits, but she, who had a lot of practice scrimping, scrimped, and assuaged her craving with the simple guava, which ranked lower in the Philippine fruit hierarchy and were therefore cheaper.

I often wondered if frugality was a sort of heredity from which one could not escape, handed down like genes, passed to one offspring and not the other. Ramon and Juanita got a small dose, Emiliana more than a heaping measure. I was not sure about Cristina; by the time I was aware, she had more money than she needed to test.

As for me, I never got it, never even learned the word. Whatever money I had ran through my fingers like water through sieve. On the other hand, my sister Clotilde cornered that market on frugality, even after her circumstances improved hugely, and she could afford whatever she wanted.

"You know," she once observed, "when you have had much practice at scrimping, you cannot bring yourself to splurge, even when later in your life you find yourself with the means to do so." Like my mother, and unlike her husband, she never bought expensive things for herself. As with the other designer items in her closet, the Ferragamos were gifts.

"Wow, look at you!" I exclaimed when we were visiting her once and she came out of her room to go to a party, elegantly clad in designer silks, her feet in Ferragamos.

"I don't know why Alfredo bothers to buy me these. I only wear them when I go formal, and how often is that?" How often indeed!

-    -   -   -

My sister had a role model in my mother. As a child, before I went to school, I remember being always barefoot. When I had to wear shoes, which was seldom, and which was always preceded by noisy protests, I remember shoes that never fit. Mother always bought them one size larger so they would still fit when my feet grew. The shoes never fulfilled Mother's expectations. With neither care on my part, nor regard for stones or water or whatever hindered my path, those shoes gave out at the seams, sprouted holes or simply gave up and just died before my feet grew into them.

Mother's one extravagance was her charities. She gave unstintingly to the church, paid tuition fees of children whose parents could not afford them, gave rice and foodstuff to those in need. And she lent money. She had a notebook in which she recorded money loaned to various people; she never asked for payment and, of course, never received any. "Why don't you just throw that notebook away," my sisters would tell her, "you never get your money back, anyway."

As a little boy, I, too, kept a notebook. For doing what I was told without giving my mother gray hairs, like taking a bath without giving Clotilde too much combat; or taking my pill without hiding it under my tongue and spitting it out when no one was looking, or not taking apart things like clocks and watches, to see how they worked until they no longer worked, Mother said she would pay me certain sums of money, the amount depending on the virtue of the deed. "Just record it in your notebook," she would say. I would take out my little notebook and, like a miser, delight in counting how much money I had, on paper. Like Mother, I never got any money from that paperwork. What I did get from that exercise was a proficiency in doing large sums in my head, like Father.

35

After dinner, I brought the jeep out. There was always a dance to celebrate the feast of saints. Fiestas proliferated in summer in our town, when school was out and the young people were home. But, by the end of June, school was already in session and this was just a small dance we were going to. I bought beer first, set the case up at the back of the jeep, picked up Paquito, and proceeded to the barrio.

The street was cordoned off. Music paraphernalia and a loudspeaker were set up at one side of the street. Barrio people had started to arrive and some of them were already dancing on the asphalt street. Later, Otic and Juan and the other cousins joined us. We never danced in these barrio dances. With drink in hand, we favored instead each other's company, watched the barrio youths spinning and gyrating and snaking down to the asphalt street to a booming rock music. Or watched an amazing tango demonstration only the young, unencumbered with inhibitions, would attempt.

"Hey, look at that," said Otic, directing our attention to a couple in exhibition mode. This was the meanest tango I saw danced on these streets. The boy was swirling the girl around and around until she looked dazed and disoriented. Then he stretched out one leg, and before she could steel herself, he pulled her up fast and close and she fell against him, straddled over his extended leg.

"Oh, Jeez," I said. We couldn't stop laughing. "That would shock the great Valentino himself."

Nights when we had places to go, transportation was not the problem. Family customs, conventions and curfews were. My parents expected our presence at dinner at 8. It was bad manners to leave the table before dinner was over and everyone was through eating. It was bad manners, too, to just plod through one's food hurriedly; we had to carry on some semblance of conversation.

My parents and the older girls spoke Spanish to each other, to the uncles and aunts, to the older cousins, but Clotilde, Ramon, and I were more comfortable chattering in the local dialect. Everyone spoke Spanish and we would answer in the dialect. Father, concerned that we might lose the Spanish tongue completely, decreed that we speak only Spanish when at table. Clotilde devised a way to spare her brains. When Father turned to her with a question, she answered with an ambiguous, "uh-huh." Short, simple, encompassing, which could mean yes, or no or maybe. This ploy forced Ramon and me to take up the gauntlet for her. All this made dinner a long drawn-out affair.

After dinner, when everyone had retired, the house had settled down for the night, and my parents were still and quiet in their room, I would sneak out, push the jeep down the driveway and out the gate, and off I would go to wherever the evening carried me. This happened several times and I was never caught. Looking back, I am sure Father was aware of these nocturnal goings on. He must have nudged Mother and said, "There he goes," and had a good laugh.

Ramon was never a party to all the shenanigans that I, Nene Escaño, Paquito Aberásturi, and Mely Sala went through. My brother was born old and responsible; drank sometimes when he was with cousins, stopped when he knew he'd had enough. He knew his own mind and spoke it, was never intimidated by anyone, always stood his ground, could not be persuaded to do anything against his better judgment, and must have thought us a bunch of idiots.

-    -   -   -

The biggest town event was the feast of the *Santo Niño*, the town's patron saint. The church, if it must be painted, was painted in time for the fiesta. Students who studied in the city, people who worked in other provinces, those who had settled on foreign shores, usually timed their vacations so that they could be home for the town fiesta. One of the prominent women of the town would serve as the *hermana mayor*. She would lead the procession carrying the statue of the *Santo Niño* that had been in the church for nobody knew how long. The church committee sometimes used a replica of the statue especially made for these processions so as not to disturb the original, or subject it to the wear and tear of being brought down, carried about and put up again. Eventually, however, they noted that it always rained on processions when the replica was used. From then on, every year the original was brought down from its high niche, dusted, garbed in new garments with laces, velvet and jewels, and was carried by the *hermana mayor* throughout the procession. Strangely after that, it never rained during the procession, even though January is traditionally a month of turbulence and storms.

On the night of the fiesta, a big dance was held in the town plaza, attended by the entire town and by people from neighboring towns as well. We were all in attendance; sometimes we ventured into the dance floor. Most times, we preferred the feel of the bottle in our hands instead, the smoky conversation, the foolish alcohol-steeped stories, Otic's *cross my heart, hope to die, true story* that most often had not happened, or had been embroidered over many times that they bore scant resemblance to what really took place; nevertheless, great laughter followed each tale, nudging the thirst for more San Migs, while the moon grew older and the night wound down to the wee hours, and we had to draw our day to a close.

Since cousins tended to mingle mostly with cousins in these affairs, Father had a rule for my sisters: if they went to these public dances, they must dance with anybody who asked them, or they could not go at all.

There was, therefore, great consternation when our uncles saw Emoy asking my sister, Juanita, to dance. One uncle fumed, "*Cualquier dia voy a permitir que una hija mia baile con un Emoy.*" ("That will be the day when I'd allow a daughter of mine to dance with an Emoy.")

I had never given him a thought before, this large, lumbering lump of a fellow, this man so of little consequence he had been working in the family business for as long as anyone could remember and yet hardly anyone seemed to know the rest of his name. He just bore a singular name, Emoy. He was one of several workers who pressed the hemp, loaded the bales on the boxcars, unloaded them onto the ships that picked up this commodity that we sell abroad, this export that had splendidly taken care of the family, taken care of the town as well, and indeed even the country.

After my uncle's indignation at the perceived impudence of a lowly worker dancing with a daughter of the family, I remembered something I had read long ago. A firm that had been in the red for a long time found itself in the black again. To reward the employees, the company president called in the workers one by one. "Jones," said the company president to one worker, "management would like you to know that it appreciates your efforts for the company. For your long and dedicated service, therefore, from now on you shall be called *Mister* Jones." Emoy never moved up to the status of *Mister*, no surprise there. Many years later, a granddaughter of Emoy married a grandson of that uncle, and I marveled at the ways Fate could slap you in the face.

36

Though we are a very close family, our fires are fanned or spent within ourselves, our emotions not usually brought out in the open. We never heard our parents quarrel. We knew things were not well with them when Mother would go home to her hometown a few kilometers away. She would come back in a couple of days, no explanations asked, none given.

This predilection for keeping private things to ourselves filtered from our parents to their children. I came home one day and Mother whispered to me, "Roy died." I had always expected Juanita to join her husband in California. She certainly had been preparing for the trip, filling chests with embroidered linens and towels and other such things women fill a hope chest with, certainly with more than just hope. The chests were left untouched and unopened for years in the room downstairs and to this day I never learned the circumstance of Roy's death.

The customary nine-day prayers for the dead were held in our house every evening, my sister grieved softly in her room, and she wore widow's weeds for one whole year.

In a gesture that was purely Juanita, she did not claim the monthly pension from the American government that she was supposed to receive as Roy's widow; she let it go instead to Roy's ailing mother, until the mother died.

Our passions are personal, sheltered in private places. Feelings are kept in guarded quarters, shielded in silence that are respected and unintruded upon, until they healed, or fizzled out, or quieted down. If they ever did.

-    -   -   -

I was away when Jacinto Aberásturi died of a heart attack, very suddenly, without warning. "*Me siento mal,*" he said. I feel bad.

Then he went to bed and very soon died.

His death shattered his wife and children, as could be expected. What we did not expect was that it shattered Father, too. Jacinto's accusations fractured their relationship, but it did not change the way Father felt for this only son of his brother. Jacinto's death devastated Father. He lashed himself at not making the first move to make peace, at letting the years pass with that silence between them, at letting those words hurt so, knowing they were not true.

Cruel words could not be called back, but they need not close doors. If they were tucked safely in some part of the memory that was seldom visited, where they could not cut like knives again, then the years could pass and that terrible word, *Ladron*! could no longer jump at you when you least expected it, like a ghost trying to spook you, *Hah*! and you did not know whether to feel outrage or be bigger than you are and turn the other way and tell yourself that what you know as untrue could not touch you, at all. Then peace could be made, silence could be breached, life could be lived as usual. Given Father's regard for family, they could. But he waited too long. And suddenly it was too late.

37

The weather was threatening outside when I woke up. The sun hid behind the clouds, dark puffs fat with rain. I went out of my room and found Mother sitting at table, waiting breakfast for us, as usual.

"Such a dark day," I said, "I hope this is not a typhoon coming up. Is the barometer dipping low?" I hoped a typhoon, which was a usual visitor in these parts, did not choose to visit on the same time I did.

"No," said Mother, "just an ordinary rainy day."

Rainy days I did not particularly mind; you cannot make things grow by spitting on them, a small boy said that in a movie once. A cliché, perhaps. But I liked it.

Typhoons are a way of life here, uninvited but expected, capricious guests that could uproot trees, transport roofs to other houses, and leave destruction behind. Trees that stay clear of their wake stand stripped afterwards, their leaves and fruits plastered on the ground. Flowers that bud and bloom vigorously in fair weather lay battered to a pulp. Rivers change courses when these typhoons come, rushing away from bridges that were built to span them, prompting one bridge inspector to send a report to his supervisor: *Bridge here, river no more!*

We had a big typhoon the last time I came home, a howler and drencher that began slowly, sure it was not welcome but still insistent, resolutely presenting itself. Clouds scudded across the sky; winds gusted. By midmorning, the clouds blackened and swirled, then the heavens opened and poured down their burden. We stood by the window and watched the river at the back of the house surging upriver instead of going down to the sea, like a mammoth snake swelling bigger as it swallowed every object that crossed its path. As the day progressed, the storm picked up speed and we listened as a crazy wind howled like a banshee, blowing coconut palms in one direction, like a row of military men with faces turned obediently to the same direction. The rains plunged in drenching sheets, lashing the windows. I looked out at the world being battered. I always stood in awe at nature when she was in a bad mood.

The wind rose and howled, snapped branches and whipped leaves from trees. We had a couple of *santol* trees, big trees that had been there for such a long time, bearing sweet fruits that we harvested by the sack and sent to cousins when they ripened. Those left over ended up in jelly jars. We had *lanzones* plants with fruits so sweet and prized, bunches hanging heavily from leafy boughs. They all ended up on the ground, shaken to a pulp by the raging wind. In its wake, the storm left hundreds of banana plants twisted and broken, too, down on the ground. Undaunted, my parents had more planted in their place.

While the winds swept rowdily outside, we waited it out inside with our books, taking stock occasionally, listening to the radio cracking and snapping out the news. Finally spent, the wind died down during the night.

The next day, I took the jeep out to assess the damage. I had always suspected a wayward streak in me, even as a boy, finding romance in high winds and tumult. I loved being out early the next morning after a stormy night. The calm *before* the storm, people always say. But the calm *after* the storm was very apt, as well. The world, stripped of leaves, was a blinding white, the morning smelled newly washed, everything stood still after the chaos in the night. I met uncles and cousins, who rose early, too, and we shared information.

By the time I returned home and we sat down to breakfast, I already had a complete report. I told Mother and my sisters which bridges were down, which houses would need repair, whose roofs had gone with the wind. "There are plenty of coconuts on the ground." Sometimes they found, among the bunch of coconuts, a *macapuno*, that aberrant coconut offspring filled entirely with meat without the usual milk.

I turned to the cook. "I guess you're going to have a busy day."

Nothing went to waste in this house. She would find ways to make use of what the typhoon had laid to waste. "The bananas are down, too," I told Mother.

"Well then," she said, as she always did when a typhoon devastated the town, "we plant again."

-    -   -   -

Today, there was nothing to do with the rains sweeping outside. This was not a typhoon by any means, but wet enough to secure us indoors. I went to the bookshelf and ran my fingers over the books, not one I hadn't read. Solace to distress, balm to ennui, spurs to flights of imagination. My gaze ranged through the titles. Today, I wanted an easy one that did not jostle my brain. Or my heart. Joseph Conrad, hmm, a dark book on a day dark as this. No, not today. F. Scott Fitzgerald, broken lives. Not that either. *The Brief Seduction of Eva*. I took the book down and opened the front page. *Dearest Juanie,* the dedication said. There were a few more lines wishing my sister a happy birthday. It was from Ed Coromina. From a time so long ago, from a time so well remembered. I stood there for a while recalling Ed's face, tried to call back Lito's, too, and Lolita's. No, not a good way to spend a rainy day. I put the book back on the shelf and resumed my search. *The Sun Also Rises*. All right, again. The book was a bit tattered; the front cover clinging precariously to the spine, testaments to the many times it had been handled, read and savored. I settled in my bed with Hemingway, once in a while tearing myself away from the book to listen to the wind shrieking outside.

By late afternoon I finished my book. I had read this book many times and each time understood why Hemingway had fallen in love with Spain, why he had written so much about this country as though it were his own. How often had I pictured Pamplona, *Iruña,* the Basques call that historical capital of the Basque country; the *San Fermines*, the running of the bulls and the bullfights; the jade-green hills, the mist-shrouded mountains, the monastery of Roncesvalles, the wild strawberries that grew on the ridge along the way to the woods and hills, the trout-filled streams up the Irati where Jake Barnes fished, the trout jumping out of numbing-cold water just waiting to be caught. How I still delighted in the glimpses Hemingway showed me of this land of my father that is in part mine, which I had read and heard so much about, through stories woven for me on nights that brewed wild as this.

38

There are people who have premonitions when something ill is going to happen. There are people who enter a place for the first time and are sure they have been there before. There are those who dream, and remember their dreams, and fear their meaning: a ghost wearing black means an estrangement from your lover, teeth falling out means death in the family. Death on the other hand is a good portent: death of a friend means a wedding (does a wedding mean the death of friendship then?); your own death signals the end of an illness. But me, I am a dolt when it comes to the dreams and the premonitions and the subtleties of life. I want the literals. I shy away from the figurative. I was planted firmly on the ground. That is why my temperament is suited to be an engineer. I trust in the constancy of numbers, where two and two always make four. I want things pinned down in black and white. I do not want gray areas in my life. Rachmaninoff and the Adagios may soothe me, but Gershwin and Porter and Kern are what really move me. I have neither the patience nor the inclination to fathom the nuances of modern art or modern poetry. Give me the romantic lyrics and sonnets anytime, where the words rhyme and their rhythms take off like wings.

You are the promised kiss of springtime
that makes the lonely winter seem long.
You are the breathless hush of evening
that trembles on a brink of a lovely song.

Jerome Kern.

Or:

Some may have blamed you that you took away
The verses that could move them on the day
When, the ears being deafened, the sight of the eyes blind
With lightning, you went from me, and I could find

Nothing to make a song about but kings
Helmets, and swords, and half-forgotten things
That were like memories of you. But now
We'll out, for the world lives as long ago;
And while we're in our laughing, weeping fit,
Hurl helmets, crowns, and swords into the pit,
But, dear, cling close to me; since you were gone,
My barren thoughts have chilled me to the bone.

William Butler Yeats.

Words like that.

The first time I saw a painting of nose upturned to the sky, I thought, *when it rains, he'll choke.* I am one of those who wondered, *what was he thinking?* when I first saw a Picasso painting of eyes and breasts in disarray, scattered here and yon. Except by that one, *Guernica,* that put my father's land on the map with the terrible strokes of his brush, I acknowledge, but stand unstirred by the genius of this great Basque. I do not see seducement and eroticism in distorted images symbolizing a woman, with its protrusions and crevices suggesting a woman's body ready to be played. I prefer the old masters, Botticelli, Raphael, Titian, and the right-in-my-face flame-haired, full-lipped, now-that-is-what-I-call-a-woman woman---a Pre-Raphaelite. I do not trust the in-betweens.

When at school I received a telegram telling me to come home, that Father had met an accident, I read it as Father had an accident. I refused to read the urgency in the message, turned my mind away from the dreaded words hidden between the lines. I blocked out the horrible possibility, the better-not-contemplated chance, the could-not-be-faced truth. Just an accident, he just wanted me there, it will be all right. Or so I wanted to believe.

When I arrived home, to a crowd gathered on the lawn, on the porch, in the living room, to a house of black-clad women, to eyes red and noses sniffling, I was still numb and steeled.

I had to see a room suffocating with flowers, my mother's and sisters' faces riven with grief, *Tio* Lorenzo standing by the coffin, his shoulders heaving, his eyes welling with tears, saying, "I just lost my right hand, my loyal companion, and my best friend."

And his coffin. And a life with him gone, that was the hardest to bear. And the tears that had hovered heavily at the back of my eyes somewhere broke out in torrents too profuse for me to contain.

- - - -

He did not have to go with the truck on that last trip, but he did. He did not have to go anymore, but he still did. This was what he did, this was what he committed to do, this was his work, this was his life, the trips and the trucks and the hemp. He was almost seventy, but physically able, mentally agile, and he just could not let go, sit on his hard-earned abundance, enjoy his old age.

The truck was top-heavy by the time they finished picking up the last bale. Their day was long as their days always were, they were on their way home, there was an oncoming vehicle. The driver swerved to avoid it. The heavy truck's wheels found soft earth. The truck tilted too far to the right, pressing my father between the full truck and a coconut tree. Just like that. A minute. A heartbeat. And his was gone. And he was gone. His chest was crushed to a pulp.

How strange the memory, and how it chooses what things to set aside ready for recall and what to keep hidden away, never to be nudged out, with no particular rhyme or order or reason. I can remember conversations said way back, remember details of long-ago events and words and looks, some with fondness, some better forgotten, some I cannot care a whit about, wondering when I do, *Now, why did I think of that?* I remember pleasures, I hoard pleasures---my first taste of imported chocolates, white nights, deserted beach, first kiss, moons peeking through palms of coconut trees, moonlight flooding the sea on nights that stir the soul, Papa with a doting look on his face, Mama dancing with Emiliana while Juanita played a waltz on the piano, favorite books, haunting songs, lingering perfumes---that conjure the sweets with which I fill my book of memories. His death rent me with grief in many places. But I cannot summon from out of there the details of his funeral. Did the skies weep when we buried him? Was there a crowd? How did the family, that most private, secluded group, bear it? To this day I cannot recall. Only that I went back to school somehow incomplete.

For a long time after that, in some quiet moments when I least expected them, bits and pieces of funereal pictures would pop up into my head, but I could not be certain whether they had really happened or they were just fragments of dreams I chose not to remember and so had lodged in some mysterious place, some recesses deep inside my brain.

In my book of memories he inhabited every page, lessons he taught ruled my life, even though I had never half-filled his shoes, large as they were. You could not be perfect, he said, nobody is; all you could do is try. Do not put too much value on financial success, but rather strive to be a decent human being, caring and kind and honest, a person with integrity. I did not lash myself then, for my weaknesses, many as they were, when I tripped, many times that I did. I was just a pupil. But I looked up to him for approbation when I tried, more times than I didn't, when I aimed higher and exceeded my grasp, when I chose the right turns when the not-so-right were always, always easier to take.

Maybe, on that next trip around, I could do better, come back more in his idea of what his son should be, more awake to what life was about, less lost to the endeavors of youth. If I believed in coming back. But I am a Catholic through and through, if I am anything, and Catholics don't believe in reincarnation, in another trip here on earth in a borrowed vessel, for a second chance at doing better. Catholics believe in an Absolute Creation. When He created me, He did not go to that discard yard and retrieve parts to make me, breathe new life in them, and say okay, here you go again. No, I was brand new. When He created me, He created me from scratch, from His own raw material that He molded to whatever He planned me to be, and gave that to my parents at my conception. I am not coming back recovered from another fallen contrivance. That other trip will not be here on earth. I believe that.

Dust thou art, to dust returnest, was not spoken of the soul.

Henry Wadsworth Longfellow.

When I leave here, I leave behind that inconsequential dust, that baggage that at last is of no more consequence. My soul will go to that purging place, to that somewhere up there where second chances are given, where credits are scored for stars earned while here on earth. Meanwhile, I could just strive to earn a few more, do a bit better, before the years run away, before youth-is-wasted-on-the-young was said of me.

In my beginning was the word. Txomin. And here came I, with many things to commend me for, and many things not.

But he did not love me any less for that, loved me anyway, totally, without conditions. I believe that, too.

39

I woke up to a perfect day. The sun streamed into my room, spilling like honey on the hardwood floor. Birds chirped, bees hummed among the flowers outside my windows. A Browning morning, *God's in His heaven, all's right with the world.*

I sat down to a breakfast of coffee, fried rice, and fish freshly caught from the sea and broiled over charcoals. We never refrigerated fish in this house. Mother hated the fishy odor she was convinced crept into everything in the fridge. "Well," Father would say, "that's how fish is. Fish smells fishy, that's its nature. Spoils rapidly, too, if not put on ice." But like everything else that conflicted with convictions ingrained in her for a long time, this simple logic went over Mother's head. Fishermen brought their catch, caught in the early dawn, directly to our house where it would skip the fridge, go straight to the kitchen and the burning charcoals or the frying pan, and then to our table. I never learned then to eat fish that had met ice, and ate fish only when I was home.

Later in the afternoon, I dressed and prepared to go out. "I guess we won't see you tonight," said Mother. She knew me well. This was the last day in a vacation that, as always, was too short.

"At least not at dinner," I said.

I took the jeep out and proceeded to the villa. Ramon Escaño, Nene's younger brother, came out from behind the house. He was a handsome, strapping boy, taller than his brother, even taller than when I saw him last.

We exchanged greetings as we entered the house. He ran up the wide staircase to the second floor, while I followed in his wake. We passed a housemaid who had been with the family for as long as there had been a family that I could recall, who had wiped runny noses, toweled dirty faces, mercurochromed bruises, down on her hands and knees, doing things to the floor, her skirt awry. "Hoy, Doray, *panapo*," Ramon said without breaking step. Cover yourself up.

"Ay, *Señorito*," she sighed, creeping out of our way, ignoring her skirt, "at my age, who'd look?" Who would, indeed.

It seemed we were surrounded by people who had grown old and shriveled serving us, for whom, like this town they were born and doubtless would die in, time stood frozen, who, despite the long years that had passed, still regarded us as children.

"I'll catch up with you," Ramon said as he proceeded to the other parts of the house.

I found Nene in his bedroom, a towel wrapped around his middle. He chattered while he got dressed. I watched him as he put on a shirt, changed his mind, took it off and threw it on the floor, searched the closet for another, shrugged himself into this one that looked like the one rejected on the floor, put on his shorts, sat down on the bed laughing at his own story, looked under the bed for his sandals, unmindful of his still disheveled state, unaware of time. He picked up a comb, swiped it a couple of times through his hair, looked at himself in the mirror, approved what he saw.

At last he was ready.

We got into the jeep and proceeded to the marketplace. Otic Escaño was already there, seated at a long table, with Juan Escaño in front of him. They looked as if they had not wasted the day. A few empty bottles stood in front of them, and a half-empty plate of *tapas*. An argument was in full swing.

"Beer?" Otic offered.

A waitress cleared the table and a fresh round of San Miguel beer and another plate of *tapas* appeared before us. Yes, Mother was right, they wouldn't see me until the wee hours tonight.

40

It was late when I got home. The town was already deep in sleep and no sound broke the melancholy silence of the night.

I parked the jeep on the driveway and watched the fireflies glow in the darker recesses of the garden, badgering the orchids under the trees, pecking them out of sleep. *Dama de noche*, the night blooming jasmine, cascaded over the garden walls like a white sheet, drenched to lushness by the recent rains. I filled my lungs with the jasmine fragrance that pervaded the night, the heavy perfume that always meant this place of my youth, that always meant Malitbog to me.

I had drunk a good deal, as I often did on nights out with my cousins, but the drink in me never clouded the pleasure I felt coming home in these cool, white dawnings. I stood solitary outside the shadows of the trees, and watched a waning moon hang lonely in the white sky, a wisp of cloud draped around its middle, with no star out, ruler of the skies tonight. The leaves trembled softly from a passing breeze, then settled back to sleep.

I emptied myself on the gardenia bushes as the white flowers looked up at me in reproach. I wondered if they would nod down tomorrow, groggy with the urined-down alcohol I showered on them, and take on a different color, borrow a different smell. Yellow-flecked white. Gardenia *con* San Miguel beer.

The house was asleep, too, when I came in. Sometimes when I came home in the early hours, one or the other of my sisters would still be awake, reading. But not tonight. The reassuring sliver of light under the door of their room was not there tonight.

Tomorrow I would be going back, to that impersonal city where I now lived, to that city where I worked and earned my living, to that city I had never called home.

But that was tomorrow.

Moonlight poured through the windows into my room. I would not be back here for a long time, and I savored this last night in this house. I undressed slowly as I watched the trees outside my window, silhouettes dark and high in the dawning sky. They would still be here when I come back, still bearing sweet fruits as they had done all these years. In my bed I settled myself to sleep, snuggling into the crisp sheets that smelled of sun. A slight wind rose and rustled softly through the avocado trees. From afar, I could hear the waves splashing onto the shore---splash, then draw, splash, then draw---weaving their music into the stillness of the night, the lullaby of leaves and waves that had comforted me since I was a boy.

Though my mind still clung to the few remaining hours of the dawn, my body was ready for repose. With the familiar strains, I slipped slowly into sleep.

41

The ship I was taking was docked on the pier. The ships used to depart this town every night. Not anymore. These days, they only come two or three times a week.

The driver lifted my bag from the jeep. "I'll take it from here," I told him as I took the bag from his hand, "thanks."

There was a time when Father would drive me to this pier when I left for school. I could still see him on that November night that June, the wind gusting high, the air threatening rain, the night black and heavy and no star in sight, that last time he saw me off. I had tarried too long in the house and the ship was about ready to leave when we arrived at the pier. He swerved the jeep and parked near the wharf's entrance.

People clustered about, bidding one another goodbye. The workers had finished loading the last of the ship's cargo.

"So," Father said, surveying me, "you're ready to do battle with those professors?"

"Like a boy scout," I said. He smiled at that.

The ship hooted its horn. They were ready to pull up the gangplank.

"Time to leave," he said. He inserted some bills, folded neatly in fours, in my shirt pocket.

"Papa," I said, shaking my head, "Mama already gave me.

"You don't want them?"

I looked at him and laughed a small laugh, not particularly happy about anything. "Thanks, Pa."

"Better go now," he said.

I patted his hand, resting there on the steering wheel, that hand that many times he spared me from the discipline he used, or threatened to use, to straighten his young children. I got out of the jeep, pulling my bag after me, and went up the gangplank.

There were always cots set aside for family members on the reserved side of the ship. I placed my bag on top of the first cot, then I leaned on the railing and looked out.

He was still there. Usually, when he was at the pier, he would be talking with the workers before the ships left.

Tonight he was just sitting there in the jeep. As though he felt me looking down at him, he looked up and I put up my hand in a half-wave. He did the same, then he nodded, swerved the jeep and drove away. That was the last time I saw him.

-     -   -   -

How long ago it all seemed! And how I still found it hard to leave; my family, my town, fraught with memories of my father.

I stood on the ship's stern as it sped away, watched the froth and foam as the ship's bottom sliced through the water, watched the lights of the town as their glitter became fainter and fainter, until they were just specks on the horizon.

Then there was only the dark night, a few stray stars, and a lump in my throat.

My thoughts went back to a time long ago. My sisters had bought him a new pair of shoes. On the way to church, without trying to avoid it, he stepped into a puddle on his path.

"Oh, Papa," said Juanita, dismayed, looking at Father's new shoes, now splattered with water.

Father looked at her. "Do you want me to take off my shoes when I see puddles on the street?"

"No," said my sister, "but... ."

"Well, then," said Father, and walked on.

And that was how he lived his life. As he did with his puddles, he saw his straight lines, walked them, never took off his shoes, and never, ever veered.

My father.

and so it ends

With rue my heart is laden
For golden friends I had
For many a rose-lipt maiden
And many a lightfoot lad

By brooks too broad for leaping
The lightfoot lads are laid
The rose-lipt girls are sleeping
In fields where roses fade.

LIV
The Shropshire Lad –
A. E. Housman

Let us raise a glass then

To this history that shaped us

To the Past

The Moving Finger writes: and having writ,
Moves on: nor all thy piety nor wit
Shall lure it back to cancel half a line,
Nor all thy tears wash out a word of it.

The Present

Ah, Love! could thou and I with Fate conspire
To grasp this sorry Scheme of Things entire,
Would not we shatter it to bits--and then
Re-mould it nearer to the Heart's Desire!

And the Future

With them the Seed of Wisdom did I sow,
And with my own hand labour'd it to grow:
And this was all the Harvest that I reap'd—
"I came like Water, and like Wind I go."

Edward FitzGerald
The Rubaiyat of Omar Khayyam

WHEN THE WORLD

WAS YOUNG

Papa, Mama
Dionisio and Mercedes Faelnar Aberásturi

Papa
Dionisio Aberásturi

Mama
Mercedes Faelnar Aberásturi

Papa with Eduardo Gonzalez
At the gold mine

Clotilde, Emiliana, Ramon, Txomin
Aberásturi

Mama, Papa
Clotilde, Emiliana
Txomin, Ramon
Aberásturi

Juanita Aberásturi

Cristina Aberásturi, Juanita Aberásturi
At school in Larrauri, Spain

Clotilde, Cristina, Juanita, Emiliana
Aberásturi

Cristina Aberásturi
Queen, Carnival of the City of Cebu, Philippines

Juanita, Roy Wonderly

Juanita Aberásturi

Emiliana Aberásturi

Emiliana Aberásturi

Clotilde Aberásturi

Clotilde Aberásturi

Ramon Aberásturi, Nene Escaño, Emiliana Aberásturi,
Txomin Aberásturi

Ramon Aberásturi

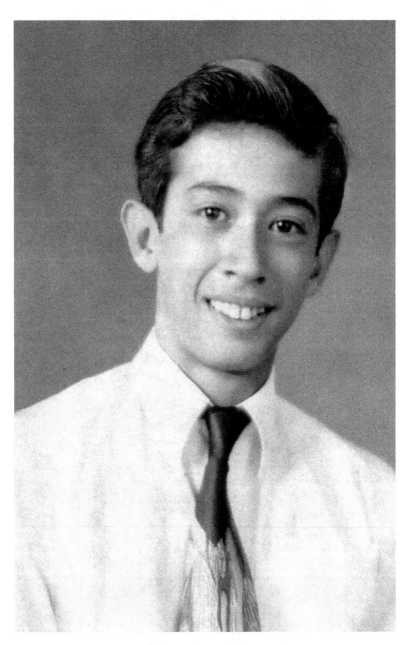

Txomin Aberásturi

Margarita Javier Escaño, Agustin Escaño

Lorenzo and Pilar Vaño Escaño
Milagros, Roque, Juan, Bingo, Ramon, Matoy, Nenita

Nenita Escaño Aberásturi
With Tony

Front: Victoria Escaño, Pilar Vaño Escaño, Basilio Urquiza
Back: Josefa Aberásturi, Margarita Aberásturi,
Father Raimundo Aberásturi, Lorenzo Escaño
Forua, Spain

Pilar Vaño Escaño, Lorenzo Escaño, Josefa Aberásturi
Father Raimundo Aberásturi, Juan Sala, Margarita Aberásturi
Eating pears in front of Aberásturi house
Forua, Spain

Victorino Aberásturi

Pacita Escaño Coromina and Victorino Aberásturi

In front of Villa Margarita
Agustin Escaño with black arm band
Malitbog, Southern Leyte, Philippines

Nenita and Chichoy Aberásturi, Otic Escaño, Matoy Escaño, a friend

Cristina Aberásturi , Carmen Aberásturi Gonzalez,
Curly Escaño Coromina
Mateo Teves, Tony Diago, Ed Escaño Coromina

SELECTED PLAYS

Sets of all plays by Agustin Escaño

The Fortune Teller
Inday Arevalo, Emiliana Aberásturi
Directed by Juanita Aberásturi Wonderly
Choreographed by Emiliana Aberásturi

Emiliana Aberásturi

Gigantes y Cabezudos
Chichoy Aberásturi and his kids
Tony, Nenette, Charito Aberásturi and Jo Coromina

Paris In Spring
Josefina Escaño, Myrna Sala, Nenette Aberásturi,
Charito Aberásturi, Evelyn Aberásturi, Fernandita Escaño

La Del Soto Del Parral
Emiliana and Juanita Aberásturi

The Authors
Nilda Aberásturi, Txomin Aberásturi

The Author
Txomin Aberásturi

The Author
Nilda Aberásturi

THE FAMILY

JUAN FAELNAR   m.   POTENCIANA ONTING

I.   AGUSTINA FAELNAR   m.   FERNANDO ESCAÑO
      15 children
   A.   JUSTINA ESCAÑO   m.   BRUNO ABERÁSTURI 3 children
       1.   Jacinto   m.   Maria Javier
       2.   Emiliana   m.   Eduardo Gonzalez
   B.   VICTORIA ESCAÑO   m.   MANUEL GONZALEZ - 3 children
   C.   PAZ ESCAÑO   m.   JOSE COROMINA - 15 children
       6.   Pacita   m.   (1)   Victorino Aberasturi
               m.   (2)   Eduardo Abad
       8.   Rosario (Curly)   m.   John Scholfield
       9.   Eduardo (Ed)   d.   1942 (?)   **m.   Lourdes (Nenita) Escaño**
      15.   Manuel (Lito)   d.   1942 (?)
   D.   AGUSTIN ESCAÑO   m.   **MARGARITA JAVIER**
       1.   Emeterio Escaño   m.   (1)   Lolita Rusca   d. 1942 (?)
                 m.   (2)   Jacinta Malaki - 5 children
   E.   LORENZO ESCAÑO   m.   PILAR VAÑO
       1.   Ramon   m.   Josefa Teves
       2.   Juan
       3.   Lourdes (Nenita)   m.   (1)   Ed Coromina   d. 1942 (?)
                (2)   Jose (Chichoy) Aberásturi
       4.   Roque   m.   Asuncion Hojas
       5.   Manuel (Matoy)   m.   Domnina Kuizon
       6.   Milagros   m.   Angel Veloso
       7.   Lorenzo, Jr. (Bingo)   m.   Josefina Tidalgo
   F.   NEMESIO ESCAÑO   m.   **ANTONINA ARELLANO** - 4 children
       1.   Fernando   m.   Felicitas Cabarubias
       2.   Fermin   m.   Josefina Pil – **9 children**
       4.   Jose (Otic)   m.   Amalia Lura
   G.   TERESA ESCAÑO   m.   **GIL GARCIA** - 4 children
       1.   Vicente   m.   Ramona Aberásturi -11 children

II.   GERARDO FAELNAR   m.   TRANQUILINA QUILA
   A.   MERCEDES FAELNAR   m.   **DIONISIO ABERÁSTURI**
       1.   Cristina   m.   Cesar Lopez
       2.   Juanita   m.   Roy Wonderly
       3.   Emiliana
       4.   Clotilde   m.   Alfredo Asuncion
       5.   Ramon   m.   Consuelo Borromeo
       6.   Txomin   m.   Nilda Anoche

I. AGUSTINA FAELNAR   m. FERNANDO ESCAÑO

   A. JUSTINA ESCAÑO   m. BRUNO ABERÁSTURI - 3 children

     1. Jacinto Aberásturi   m. Maria Javier

       1) Vicente   m. Rosenda Aguelo
       2) Ramona   m. **Vicente Garcia**
       3) Bruno   m. Concepcion Sescon
       4) Jose (Chichoy)   m. **Lourdes (Nenita) Escaño**
       5) Agustina   m. Zosimo Veloso
       6) Carmen   m. Jesus Ortega
       7) Francisco (Paquito) m. Miren Milagroso
       8) Justina
       9) Jacinto, Jr.   m. Evelyn Reeves
      10) Margarita   m. Antonio Centeno

     2. Emiliana Aberásturi   m. Eduardo Gonzalez

       1) Jose Mari   m. Hazel Graham
       2) Carmen   m. Mateo Teves
       3) Pilar   m. Carlos Aldanese

   B. VICTORIA (Toyang) ESCAÑO m. MANUEL GONZALEZ

   C. PAZ ESCAÑO   m. JOSE COROMINA

     6. Pacita   m. (1) Victorino Aberásturi
                           m. (2) Eduardo Abad

     8. Rosario (Curly) Coromina - Iliff David Richardson
       1) Velma
                    m. John Scholfeld

     9. Eduardo (Ed) Coromina d. 1942 (?)
                    m. Lourdes (Nenita) Escaño
       1) Josephine   m. Ron Swigert
     15. Manuel (Lito) Coromina d. 1942 (?)

   D. AGUSTIN ESCAÑO   m. MARGARITA JAVIER

     1. Emeterio Escaño   m. (1) Lolita Rusca d. 1942 (?)
       1) Agustin, Jr. (Nene) m. Felicula Cruz
       2) Ramon   m. Maria Pilar Picornell

                   m. (2) Jacinta Malaki

E. LORENZO ESCAÑO m. **PILAR VAÑO**

1. Ramon Escaño m. **Josefa Teves**
  1) Ramon
  2) Alejandro
  3) Maria Antonia

2. Juan Escaño

3. Lourdes (Nenita) Escaño
                              m. (1) **Ed Coromina** d. 1942 (?)
  1) Josephine
                              m. (2) Jose (Chichoy) Aberasturi
  2) Rosa
  3) Charito
  4) Nenette
  5) Ramon
  6) Milagros
  7) Lourdes
  8) Antonio
  9) Lorenzo
  10) Jacinto
  11) Consuelo

4. Roque Escaño m. **Asuncion Hojas**
  1) Isidro

5. Manuel Escaño (Matoy) m. **Domnina Kuizon**
  1) Clemente
  2) Gabriel
  3) Manuel
  4) Maria Irene
  5) Leo
  6) Lorenzo

6. Milagros Escaño m. **Angel Veloso**
  1) Angel, Jr.
  2) Lorenzo
  3) Marison
  4) Mercedes
  5) Josefa
  6) Tomas
  7) Clementina

7. Lorenzo Escaño, Jr. (Bingo)   m. Josefina Tidalgo
  1) Antonio
  2) Josefina
  3) Lorenzo III
  4) Pilar Geraldine

F. NEMESIO ESCAÑO   m. **ANTONINA ARELLANO**
  1. Fernando Escaño   m. **Felicitas Cabarubias**
    1) Fernandita
    2) Nemesio
    3) Jesus
  2. Fermin Escaño   m. **Josefina Pil**
  3. Carmen Escaño   m. 1) **James Fox**
       2) **Arno Duchstein**
  4. Jose (Otic) Escaño   m. Amalia Lura
    1) Joselito
    2) Roberto
    3) Grace
    4) Fernando
       CRISTINA BARCELON - 8 children

G. TERESA ESCAÑO   m. **GIL GARCIA**
  1. Vicente Garcia   m. Ramona Aberásturi - 11 children

II. GERARDO FAELNAR   m.   TRANQUILINA QUILA

    A.   **MERCEDES FAELNAR**   m.   **DIONISIO ABERÁSTURI**

        1.   **Cristina Aberásturi**   m.   **Cesar Lopez**

           1)   Maria Cristina

           2)   Cesar

           3)   Dionisio

           4)   Mercedes

           5)   Maria Ana

           6)   Pilar

           7)   Gerardina

        2.   **Juanita Aberásturi**   m.   **Roy Wonderly**

        3.   **Emiliana Aberásturi**

        4.   **Clotilde Aberásturi**   m.   **Alfredo Asuncion**

           1)   Ines

           2)   Alfredo

           3)   Hernan

           4)   Eva

           5)   Lisa

        5.   **Ramon Aberásturi**   m.   **Consuelo Borromeo**

           1)   Nicolo

           2)   Maria Raisa

           3)   Anton

           4)   Cristina Mercedes

        6.   **Txomin Aberásturi**   m.   **Nilda Anoche**

           1)   Dionisio

           2)   Jose Rene

           3)   Domingo Jose Antonio

           4)   Maria Mercedes

           5)   Gerardo

           6)   Jose Maria

           7)   Maria Teresa

           8)   Martin Antonio

GEOLOGICAL TREE OF
MERCEDES FAELNAR AND DIONISIO ABERÁSTURI

A. MERCEDES FAELNAR m. DIONISIO ABERÁSTURI

1. **Cristina Aberásturi m. Cesar Lopez**
   1) Maria Cristina - m. Eugenio A. Picazo
      a. Cristine Pilar - m. Alexander Reichert
         Nicolas Martin, Katerina Marie, Isabel Sofia
      b. Anna Cecilia - m. Grahan Churchley
         Natalie Anne, James & Philip (twins)
      c. Leopoldo Jose Maria
      d. Cesar Francisco - m. Erica Sulit
         Sofia Maria
      e. Rosario Teresa
   2) Cesar, Jr. - m. Margarita Reyes
      a. Cesar Anthony
      b. Czarina Margarita
   3) Dionisio - m. Sylvia Heras
      a. Antonio - m. Jenny Suarez
      b. Carlos - m. Minette Tirona
      c. Ines - m. Jerome Matti
      d. Celine
      e. Isabel
                    m. Honeylyn Tom
      f. John Paul
   4) Mercedes - m. Luis Gaston
      a. Stephanie - m. William Lawrence
      b. Cesar Louie - m. Antoinette Fleta
      c. Cristina Mercedes
      d. James Benjamin
   5) Maria Ana - m. Freddie W. Zayco
      a. John Abraham
      b. Ronald Anthony
      c. Thomas Andrew
      d. Victoria Ann
   6) Pilar - m. Alfonso Y. Quiros
      a. Angela
      b. Alexandra
      c. Miguel
      d. Victoria
      e. Elena

7) Gerardina - m. Adolfo Aguirre
   a. Juan Antonio
   b. Elizabeth Marguerite
   c. Michelle Gabrielle
2. **Juanita Aberásturi   m.   Roy Wonderly**
3. **Emiliana (Lily) Aberásturi   d. 1/23/84**
4. **Clotilde Aberásturi   m.   Alfredo Asuncion**
   1) Ines Victoria - m. Rolando Viray
      a. Jose Marco
      b. Jose Martin
   2) Alfredo Wenceslao, Jr. - m. Roxanne Romero
      a. Miguel Antonio
   3) Hernan Alvaro - m. Joanna Llorca
      a. Carlos Lorenzo
      b. Nicholas
      c. Christina Anna
   4) Eva - m. Jose Miguel Yulo
      a. Regina Victoria
      b. Mariel Alexandra
      c. Jesus Miguel
   5) Lisa Mercedes - m. John Feliciano
5. **Ramon Aberásturi   m.   Consuelo Borromeo**
   1) Nicolo - m. Paula Zayco
      a. Ainara
      b. Domeka
   2) Maria Raisa - m. Zoilo Velez
      a. Tomas
      b. Luis
   3) Anton
   4) Cristina Mercedes - m. Fernando Ducloux

6. **Txomin Aberásturi** d. **5/10/07**
   m. **Nilda Anoche**
   1) Dionisio - m. Elsie Castro
      a. Dominic
      b. & c. Silvia Mercedes & Sofia Mercedes (twins)
      d. Maria Bianca
   2) Jose Rene - m. Vivien Quilisadio
      a. Erno
      b. Chomin
   3) Domingo Jose Antonio - m. Margarita Trageco
      a. Isabel Patricia
      b. Beatrice Teresa
      c. Domingo Jose Antonio
   4) Maria Mercedes - m. Roberto Nuñez
      a. Kevin Christopher
   5) Gerardo Pedro
   6) Jose Maria
   7) Maria Teresa (Maitechu) - m. Jon Plamenco
      a. Alessandra
      b. Giovanna
   8) Martin Antonio - m. Iasia McCord
      a. Martin Anthony
      b. Iasia Maria
      c. Alicia Michelle

I have many to thank

Susan Malone, first to edit this book in its infancy,
whose high praises for the way I write kept me going,
despite and still.

Susan Astor, great editor and dear friend.

My niece, Nina Hagel, who read, edited, critiqued
and unselfishly spared time for me.

My nephew, Edgar Servando, my computer is
lost without you.

My niece, Mila Aberásturi, for her expert help
with emails to and from Malitbog.

My daughter-in-law, Marge Aberásturi, computer
expert herself.

Ramon Ferreira and Nigel Manalili, who did wonders
with the old, spotted pictures.

James Wasvary, esteemed brother-in-law,
whose opinions I always value.

Juanita Aberásturi Wonderly and Ramon Aberásturi -
without your unwavering support I could not have
finished this book.

I am grateful.

HALF-FORGOTTEN THINGS
Vignettes From A Life

A Memoir

By

Txomin Aberásturi
&
Nilda Aberásturi

New York
May 2010

Printed in the USA
CPSIA information can be obtained
at www.ICGtesting.com
LVHW010758220823
755864LV00035B/249